KITCHENS

Jane Moss Snow

National Association of Home Builders
15th & M Streets NW
Washington, DC 20005

Kitchens

ISBN 0-86718-278-4
Library of Congress Card Number 86-63287

15th and M Streets NW
Washington, DC 20005

When ordering this publication, please provide the following information:

Title
ISBN 0-86718-278-4
Price
Quantity
NAHB membership number (as it appears on the *Builder* or *Nation's Building News* label)
Mailing address (including street number and zip code)

Cover photos were provided by St. Charles Manufacturing Company (top left photo), West and Associates (bottom left photo), and Wood-Mode Cabinetry (right photo).

Jane Moss Snow

Author of KITCHENS

About the Author

Kitchens author Jane Moss Snow is a respected home builder, interior designer, and author.

From 1972 to 1978, Ms. Snow was president of DWS Enterprises, Inc., a home building company that constructed single-family residences in New York and Virginia. During this period, Ms. Snow, a cooking authority, published *A Family Harvest* (Bobbs Merrill), which was chosen as a *Better Homes & Gardens* Cookbook of the Month in 1976.

Ms. Snow also presided over her own interior design business in New York and Southampton. She studied at the New York School of Interior Design and apprenticed with Clifford Stanton Interiors of New York.

In addition, Ms. Snow was Director of Public Affairs for Home Owners Warranty Corporation (HOW) from 1978 to 1985. She is an authority on construction quality control and HOW's warranty insurance program for new single-family homes.

Ms. Snow has been an interior design feature writer for the Gannett News Service, serving 90 newspapers nationwide. Her articles have also appeared in *National Geographic, Parade Magazine, Mortgage Banker, Mid-Atlantic Country, Medical Economics,* and *Challenge!*

National Association of Home Builders
15th & M Streets, N.W.
Washington, D.C. 20005

Contents

Acknowledgments

Kitchens was produced under the general direction of Kent Colton, NAHB Executive Vice President, and by the following NAHB staff members: William D. Ellingsworth, Senior Staff Vice President, Public Affairs; Denise L. Darling, Senior Staff Vice President, Publishing Services; Susan D. Bradford, Director of Publications; Ann Elizabeth Gilmore, Publications Editor; and David Rhodes, Art Director. Martin Mintz, NAHB Director of Technical Services, was the technical reviewer of the book. Timothy P. Fennell provided the drawings for *Kitchens*.

The author also acknowledges the Whirlpool Corporation and the National Kitchen and Bath Association for their cooperation; and Don O'Connor, of Wood-Mode Cabinetry; and J. Fredric Simms, Assistant Librarian, Washington Gas Light Company.

In addition, the following organizations provided the photographs appearing in the book:

Armstrong World Industries, Inc.
P.O. Box 3001
Lancaster, PA 17604

Broan Manufacturing Company, Inc.
Hartford, WI 53027

Color Design Art
17315 Sunset Boulevard
Pacific Palisades, CA 90272

Frigidaire, WCI Appliance Group
300 Phillipi Road
Columbus, OH 43228

General Electric Company
Major Appliance Group
Appliance Park
Louisville, KY 40225

Godfrey & Associates of Orlando, Inc.
329 Park Avenue South
Winter Park, FL 32789

Hot Point Division
General Electric Company
Major Appliance Group
Appliance Park
Louisville, KY 40225

Jenn-Air Company
3035 N. Shadeland
Indianapolis, IN 46226

Kohler Company
Kohler, WI 53044

The Maytag Company
Newton, IA 50208

Moen Group-Stanadyne, Inc.
377 Woodland Avenue
Elyria, OH 44035

Quaker Maid
Route 61
Leesport, PA 19533

Siematic Corporation
P.O. Box 7286
Feasterville, PA 19047

St. Charles Manufacturing Co.
1611 East Main Street
St. Charles, IL 60174

Sub-Zero Freezer, Inc.,
11 West Illinois Street
Chicago, IL 60610

Summitville Tiles, Inc.
Summitville, OH 43962

Thermador/Waste King
5119 District Boulevard
Los Angeles, CA 90040

Washington Gas Light Company
6801 Industrial Road
Springfield, VA 22151

Whirlpool Corporation
2000 U.S. Highway 33 North
Benton Harbor, MI 49022

Wilsonart Laminated Plastics Company
600 General Bruce Drive
Temple, TX 76501

Wood-Mode Cabinetry
Kreamer, PA 17833

Chapter 1

Introduction

All of the efforts of early man revolved around the fireside, the glowing embers that browned meat and turned grains into breads.

Today's hearth—the kitchen—remains a focal point for family activities. Gourmet cooks and microwave devotees alike consider the kitchen a central part of the home. Its beauty and utility are a source of pride as well as practicality.

The kitchen's central role makes it a key design element and a major selling point in a home. In a 1985 nationwide survey of builders, 82.5 percent of respondents rated the kitchen as a critical factor in the home-buying decision (*Kitchen and Bath Design News* 1985). Builders recognize good design and amenities as key elements in the kitchen. Moreover, 52.5 percent of all builders/developers design the kitchens in the new homes they build, according to the same survey.

The day when a builder took a floor plan to a kitchen supply company and said, "Give me something that looks colonial," has passed, along with avocado and harvest gold. Now, a kitchen must complement the overall ambience of a house and suit the life-style of the intended market.

To design a good kitchen, you must first ask: What is my market? Is it the first-time home buyer, with specific needs, who accounts for about 40 percent of new home purchases? Or is it the vast and increasingly well-heeled, move-up market? Or is the target the fastest-growing segment of all, the empty-nesters? And if so, what segment of that market? After all, empty-nesters may be active 55-year-olds still working or retirees or senior citizens in their 70's. This market will grow a hefty 23.3 percent in the 1980's alone.

After determining your segment of the market, learn what the consumer wants. Never before has the market been so educated or affluent, allowing consumers to choose a home that has aesthetic appeal, rather than just a roof over their heads.

A vast amount of information exists today on consumer appeal and preferences. Good design is no longer a matter of guesswork; it is the product of careful, thorough studies by specialists who have analyzed everything from the proper height of a cabinet to the space needed beside a cook top for a pot handle. New, exciting advances have been made in cabinetry and appliances. Home buyers today are aware, through the media, of exotic finishes, hand-painted tiles, electronic controls, and faucets that adjust to various heights. The consumer wants top-of-the-line fixtures and appliances, the best quality in cabinets, plenty of storage space—and custom touches.

To attract your market is an immense challenge. This manual will help in meeting that challenge.

Whether you design the plan or work with an interior designer, careful planning—even before the studs are erected—can save both time and money and ensure that the finished product satisfies the needs of the market.

Chapter 2

Consumer Preferences

You don't need to rely on guesswork to find out what the consumer wants. Surveys are constantly being conducted to determine consumer preferences in everything from appliances to amenities. Although surveys may differ in percentages, the overall results serve as excellent guides.

In the 1985 NAHB study, *Decisions for the '90's*, consumers named the relationship of kitchen to family room as the most important feature in kitchen design. The overwhelming choice was a kitchen that is visually open to the family room, with some type of division. Almost 46 percent of those surveyed chose this layout. Side-by-side placement of kitchen and family room with a wall divider was chosen by 21 percent of those surveyed. Only 17.4 percent chose completely separated areas, while 15.8 percent preferred completely open kitchen/family rooms (National Association of Home Builders 1985).

Table 1 - Preferred Kitchen/Family Room Arrangement

Preferred Design	*Percentage of Respondents*
Visually open with divider	45.9
Side-by-side but with a wall	20.9
Completely separate areas	17.4
Completely open	15.8

The open design makes a home look larger. Although the American Restaurant Association reports that more people are eating out, the home buyer wants a kitchen twice as big as his present one. If you are working with limited square footage, imaginative use of room dividers creates the illusion of much more space.

The consumer's desire for quality is reflected in every study. What were luxuries a few years ago are becoming standard equipment, and builders are finding that the consumer is willing to pay for the extra quality. Quality workmanship is important to 96 percent of home buyers. Of the 10 features considered most important by consumers in selecting a new home, 8 relate to quality. Floor plan and layout are rated very important by 81 percent of the respondents, with quality of paint and floor tiles high on the list (National Association of Home Builders 1985).

The majority of respondents cited cooking and informal eating as the most important household activity affecting house design. What does this mean to you? It means that a well laid-out kitchen with high-quality products and amenities can be the difference between a fast sale and a slow one.

Surveys by NAHB and other industry organizations have produced a comprehensive list of specific consumer preferences. (See Figure 1.) For example, more cabinet storage space is first on the consumers' wish list. More counter space ranks second and a more functional layout, third (National Association of Home Builders 1985).

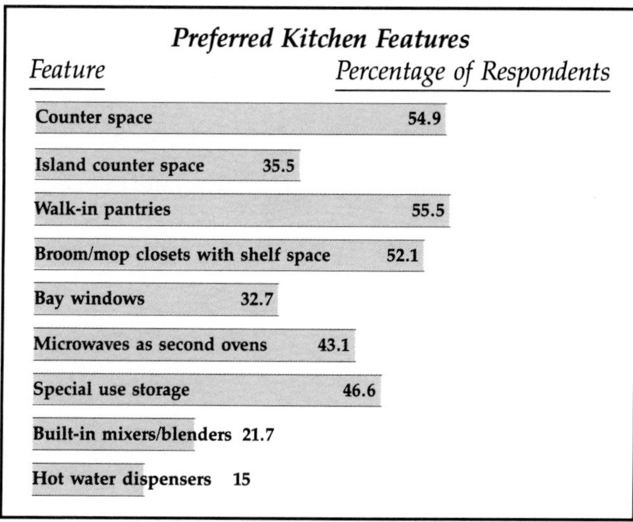

Figure 1. Preferred Kitchen Features

Consumers surveyed in a 1984 study conducted by *Kitchen and Bath Business* expressed the following preferences:

- 82 percent opted for double bowl sinks
- 73.4 percent chose stainless steel sinks
- Pull-out shelves, lazy susans, breadboards, cutlery dividers, bread boxes, and spice racks were the most popular interior fittings for cabinets
- 59 percent selected resilient vinyl floors
- 79 percent chose selected laminated countertops; (In the luxury market, 59 percent of respondents selected laminate; 23 percent chose tile; 18 percent opted for Corian.)

The demand is also high for desk/planning areas and for eat-in space/counter seating. In the luxury market, 36 percent want planning areas, and 18 percent want counter seating (*Kitchen and Bath Business* 1984). Knowledge of consumer preferences is essential for building marketable kitchens. This knowledge, applied along with the design principles presented in the following chapters, assures the success of your kitchens—and your home sales.

Courtesy Quaker Maid

Figure 2. An open design makes a home look larger.

Chapter 3

The Well-Designed Kitchen

The kitchen is a working room; it serves a specific function, and its design should make work as effortless and efficient as possible. Observe the number of steps required by the cook in your family. Is he or she making two moves where one could have been made? Are counters poorly arranged, causing the cook extra steps? When groceries are brought in from the car, is the door close by the refrigerator counter so that putting the food away is easy? Or must groceries be lugged halfway across the room?

Take a look at a picture of an old-fashioned kitchen. (See Figure 3.) It is difficult to imagine cooking for a large number of people in the typical pre-World War II kitchen because of the inconvenience involved. Design has made great strides since those days, both aesthetically and practically.

The modern kitchen cabinet has taken over, a blessing in convenience and in good looks. Appliances are constantly being improved, and new inventions such as the disposal and microwave add conveniences unheard of 50 years ago.

In addition, scientific studies of good kitchen design have determined the best layouts, the most comfortable heights and placements of equipment, and proper ventilation and lighting, all factors that separate the so-so kitchen from the well-designed one.

While it was once quite expensive to afford a decent kitchen, today even a basic home can have a well-designed kitchen that functions efficiently, providing emotional gratification for the home owner and a good reputation for the builder.

Getting the best layout from the available space requires thoughtful planning. Often, the shifting of a door or the addition of a few feet makes the difference between a well-designed, workable room and one in which the refrigerator protrudes inconveniently.

Planning at the blueprint stage keeps down costs. Whether working with an interior designer or designing the kitchen yourself, this is the time to consider good design. Will a bay or greenhouse window add appeal? Can a breakfast area be included? Will a room divider work better as an eating counter or a combination cook top and counter?

If you're not working with an interior designer, you can often find professional help through a kitchen supply manufacturer. If you decide to work with a designer, one way to ensure professionalism is to find one who belongs to the Society of Certified Kitchen Designers (CKD). Their members have met rigid requirements and are experts in the field.

Whether employing a designer or not, your understanding of the principles of good design is essential. The basic rules of kitchen design will assist you in analyzing floor plans and critiquing design suggestions.

The Basic Rules in Kitchen Design

First, the kitchen should have *easy access* from other parts of the house and the garage. It should also be easily accessible from the dining room, the family and play areas, the exterior of the house, and the car.

The covered dish was invented to keep food warm while it was carried from the kitchen to the dining room. Today, we don't have to suffer this inconvenience. Food can be moved from stove to table in a flash if easy access is planned for.

Little children playing on the kitchen floor is a dangerous practice. Now, busy cooks can keep an eye on children through open designs that combine the kitchen with the living areas. Most women prefer homes with a kitchen and a great room or other room combined but visually separated. This design works equally well for families without children who enjoy being together. Isolation in the kitchen is a thing of the past.

The consumer also wants easy access from the kitchen to the exterior so that groceries can be unloaded from the car with the least possible lugging. The door from the carport or garage should open into or beside the kitchen.

In addition, an exterior door to the patio, lawn, or deck should be convenient to the kitchen for ease in entertaining and for the comfort of the family. Children playing in the yard should be able to use the refrigerator without running through the entire house. Also, a layout that provides access and visibility enables mothers to watch children in the backyard.

The second basic rule of kitchen design is to carefully plan for *traffic patterns*. If possible, no one should have to pass through the working part of the kitchen to reach any part of the house or to get outdoors. This is the safest arrangement because children (and adults) avoid bumping into the stove and spilling hot pans.

The kitchen is an arrangement of *work centers*, and proper arrangement of these centers is the third basic rule in kitchen design. Scientific studies have measured the functions performed in the kitchen and have determined that work centers should be carefully related to save time and energy, while increasing pleasure in using the room.

Each work center has a specific function, requires its own equipment, and is complete in itself. The three primary work centers are the clean-up center, the refrigerator center, and the cooking center.

The clean-up center is the one most commonly used, accounting for 40 to 47 percent of the work done in the kitchen. The cooking center accounts for 22 to 29 percent, and the mixing area, 11 to 15 percent of the

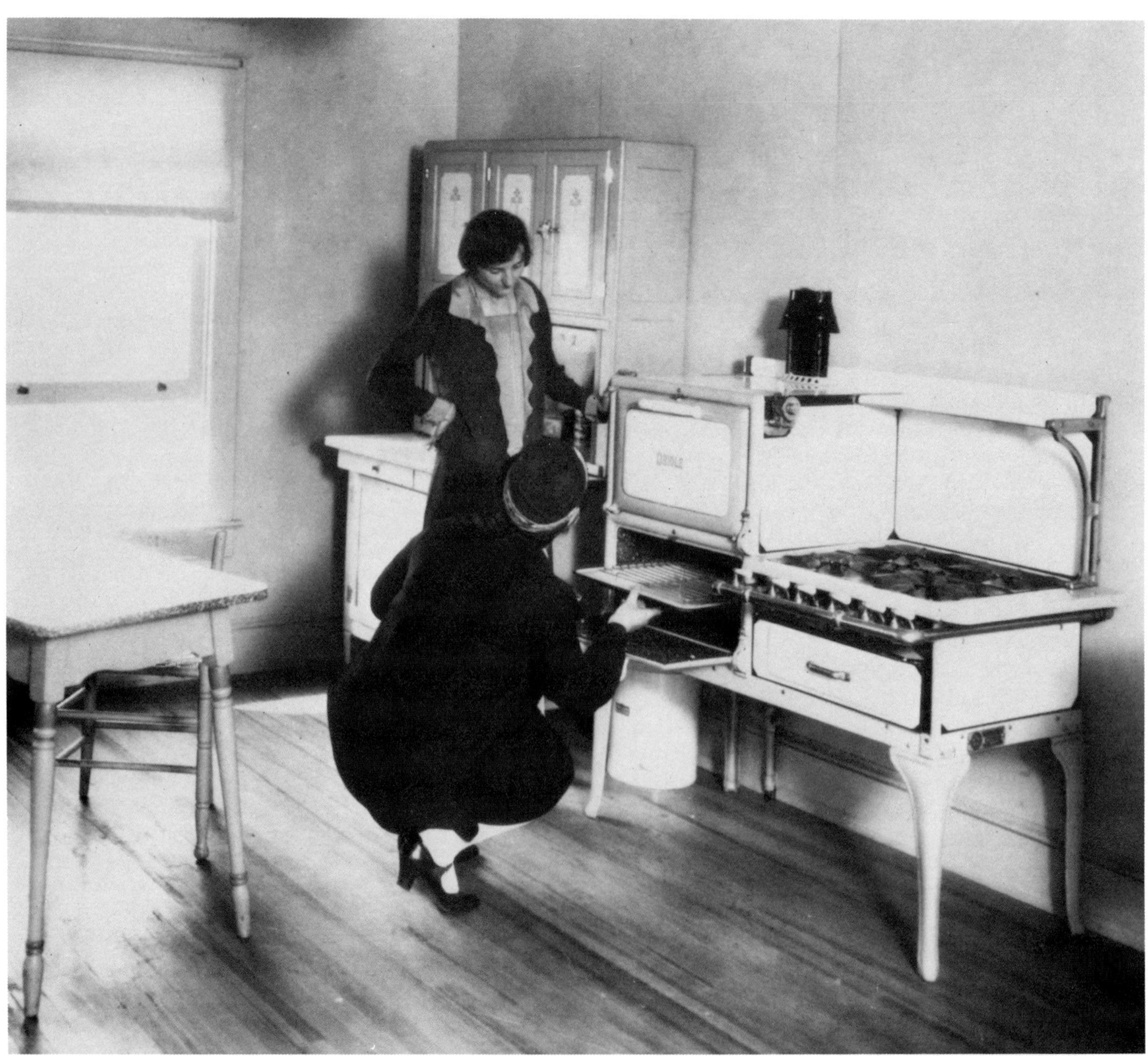

Courtesy Washington Gas Light Company

Figure 3. Old-fashioned kitchens were large but inefficient.

work, according to a definitive 1965 study by the Small Homes Council - Building Research Council (National Kitchen and Bath Association 1984).

The secondary work centers are the mixing center and the serving center.

Although these are the five traditional centers, consumers are demanding a sixth: the eating center. Whether this is a separate area or a counter or both, it should be included in basic planning for the kitchen.

Furthermore, buyers of upscale homes want a planning center, including a desk, some bookshelves, drawer space, and even a computer center. Entertainment centers with secondary sinks, refrigerators, and cabinetry for bars comprise an additional center.

The following describes the work centers and discusses their best arrangement.

Primary Work Centers

The clean-up center, the sink and the dishwasher, serves a preparation function (vegetable cleaning) and a clean-up function.

The refrigerator center provides fresh and frozen food storage. This center includes counter space on which to place bagged groceries prior to storage and foods removed for use.

The cooking center includes the cook top, microwave, and/or regular oven, as well as counter space for pans and casseroles when they are removed from the cook top or ovens.

Secondary Work Centers

The mixing center is the counter space used in food preparation. It should be located between the clean-up center and the refrigerator for ease in getting food from the refrigerator and clean-up at the sink. The space requires access to mixers, blenders, food processors, knives/cutlery, bowls, platters, pans, cookie sheets, casseroles, foods, and pantry storage of canned goods. This is an ideal location for the microwave, which can be installed under the cabinets, saving counter space.

The serving center is related to the cooking center and should be located next to the cook top, large enough to hold plates and serving dishes. Ideally, it is close to an eating area; it may also be a part of a counter eating arrangement.

Other Centers

The eating center, where people may sit and eat, may be the end of a peninsula counter, part of an island, or a counter located by a pass-through. It may be a built-in table and bench (banquette) or space for a table and chairs. Some large kitchens include a small counter eating area plus table space.

The planning center may include a desk and bookshelves, which cabinet manufacturers are now featuring in their lines. Telephone jacks and lighting must be provided for planning areas, which should generally be placed at the end of cabinet runs. Otherwise, they may interfere with the working part of the room.

Courtesy Armstrong World Industries, Inc.

Figure 4. This move-up kitchen has both planning and eating centers.

Courtesy Wood-Mode Cabinetry

Figure 5. The peninsula in this kitchen has an entertainment center with a sink, bar, and wine bottle storage.

The entertainment center, appropriate in spacious rooms, may contain a sink with a bar faucet, a small refrigerator set in a cabinet; cabinets for glassware and bottles add to the sales appeal. (See Figure 5.)

These centers must be located away from the primary work centers and convenient to the living areas of the home.

Courtesy Sub-Zero Freezer Company, Inc.

Figure 6. This kitchen has an efficient work triangle.

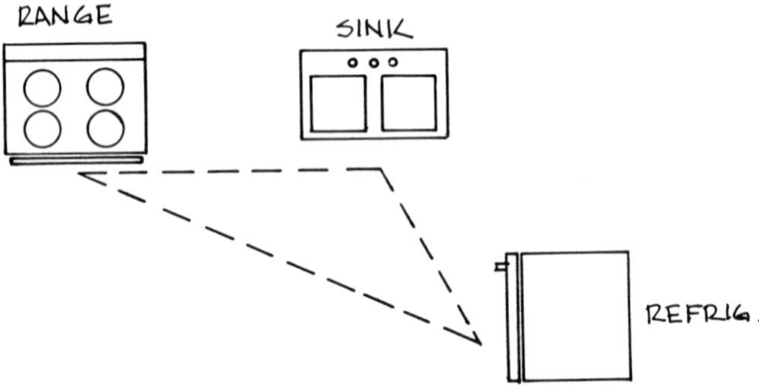

Figure 7. The Work Triangle

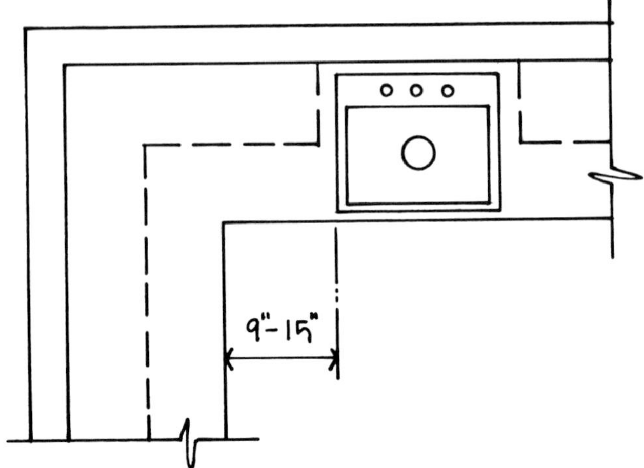

Figure 8. Allow a minimum clearance of 9 to 15 inches between the sink and the return counter.

The Work Triangle

Once you have identified the work centers in your kitchen design, the spatial relationship of these centers to each other and to the remainder of the house is the next consideration for a well-designed kitchen.

The primary work centers—the clean-up center, the refrigerator, and the range/cook top—should form a triangle. These basic appliances are best positioned so that the user functions with the fewest possible steps between each point of the triangle. Each center also needs its adjacent workspace, so a good design plans for the mixing center. The serving center is beside the range, and the eating and planning centers are located conveniently outside the triangle.

In the most efficient layout, the sink forms the apex of the work triangle and is equidistant from the other two primary work centers, the refrigerator and the cook top. The arms of the triangle should not be less than 12 feet nor exceed 22 feet. (The absolute maximum is 26 feet.) Each arm may vary, of course, but in the 12-foot kitchen, the arms might be 4 feet X 4 feet X 4 feet, and in the 22-foot kitchen, they might be 6-1/2 feet X 7-1/2 feet X 8 feet. Ideally, the individual legs are between 4 and 7 feet long. (See Figure 7.)

Because it's the most used center, the sink forms the basis for planning the entire kitchen. The sink may be either a single, double, or triple. Sinks are now available with fitted cutting boards, crockery baskets, drainers, as well as built-in waste disposal chutes. Offset drain holes allow for offset disposal installation in the cabinet below, increasing storage space.

Place the sink under a window if possible. Generally, it is centered, but if placed off-center, adjust the arrangement of cabinet doors and the countertop to compensate aesthetically. Allow a clearance of 9 to 15 inches between a corner sink and the return counter. (See Figure 8.)

The dishwasher, located adjacent to the sink, is a part of the clean-up center and should be to the left of the sink for right-handed people. The disposal and the trash compactor are also part of the clean-up center. Allow a minimum of 20 inches of countertop for loading when the dishwasher is not placed next to the sink. Too often, dishwashers are placed at right angles to the sink or adjacent to a corner, so that it is difficult to stand at the sink to load and unload. Allow a minimum of 48 inches between the front of the dishwasher and any structure opposite. This is the clearance needed to open the door and allow passage. Place the dishwasher away from corners or other appliances (including protruding drawer handles) that will prevent the free opening of the door. Leave at least 3 inches between the edge of the door and another cabinet. (See Figures 9 and 10.)

The clean-up center should provide space for the following:

- Bins for storing such things as potatoes that

need washing but not refrigeration

- Vegetable brushes, knives, spoons, and utensils
- Lettuce spinners and strainers
- Cleaning supplies
- Disposal, trash compactor, and wastebasket

The second primary work center, the refrigerator, is best located next to the door where groceries are brought in from the car. It should be placed toward the end of the counter run and, for right-handed people, on the right-hand end of the counter.

Install the refrigerator so that the door opens away from the countertop where food is placed for mixing. (See Figure 11.) Right-handed people want doors to open to the right. Custom-built kitchens for left-handed people should feature a left-opening door. Allow adequate clearance for the door opening. A refrigerator is generally 29 inches from front to back, deeper than the standard 24-inch cabinet. Add to that the width of the door. Include enough room to open doors to their stops or past to permit removal of shelves and hydrators. Remember that the average refrigerator is deeper than the standard 24-inch cabinet.

Traditionally, refrigerators have not been placed beside stoves, cook tops, or ovens, although with today's insulation this requirement is obsolete. Still, this is not the best layout.

Clearance for a side-by-side refrigerator is 12 inches on the left-hand side and 18 inches on the right, between the unit and the end wall.

Provide sufficient counter space beside the refrigerator to place groceries for unloading and storage. (This area may also be the mixing center.) Side-by-side refrigerators should have counter space on each side, if possible. (See Figure 12.)

Separate freezers need not be placed beside refrigerators and should be out of the work triangle; a utility area is a good location.

Place the cook top/range, the third primary work center, closest to the dining area to minimize steps in serving food. Allow enough area between the range and the end wall to permit door swing. (See Figures 13 and 14.) With built-in appliances, more flexibility is possible. The cook top can be placed on an island or counter in the work triangle. The oven can then be placed in another part of the triangle or slightly removed from it. The cook top should be a part of the work triangle, however, with the sink and mixing center.

For built-in ovens at eye level, allow at least 36 inches of clearance from the front of the oven for the door to open. This permits someone to stand in front of the oven with the door open. Double check the door size if the appliance is not standard. The oven bottom should be 3 inches below shoulder height. Make sure there is enough clearance on the side if the oven's installed near a return wall.

When installing free-standing ranges, allow 48 inches between the front of the stove and any structure opposite to permit the door to open while someone stands in front of it with room for another person to get by. Walking space requires 60 inches. (See Figure 15.)

Install cook tops on an exterior wall, if possible, to ease ducting to the outside. Do not install a cook top next to a vertical wall return, and leave 12 to 15 inches

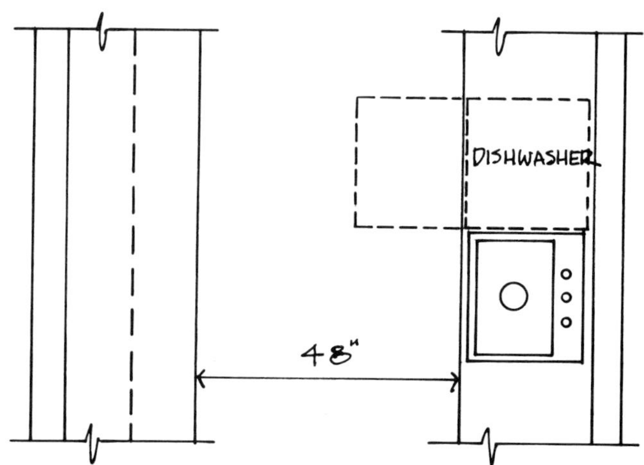

Figure 9. Place the dishwasher to the left of the sink, leaving 48 inches of clearance, which allows for the dishwasher door opening and for someone to edge by.

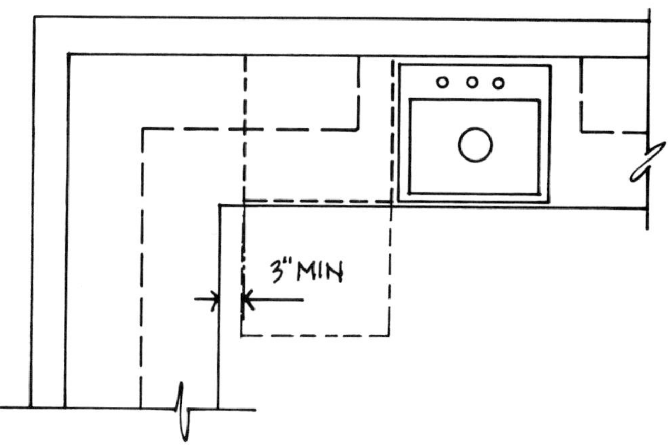

Figure 10. Allow at least 3 inches of clearance from the dishwasher door opening to the return counter.

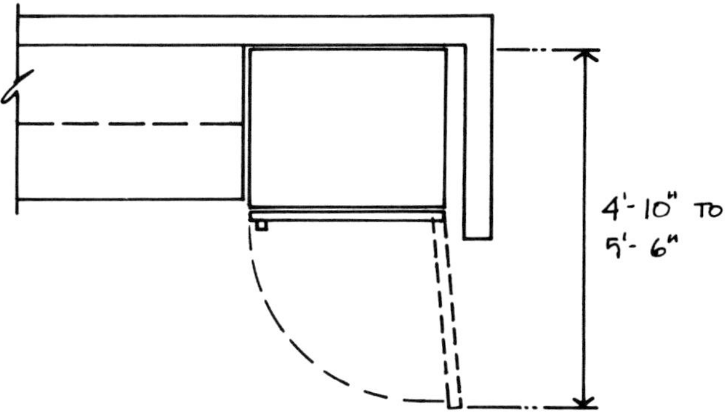

Figure 11. The refrigerator door should open away from the countertop and have enough clearance to open past the stop.

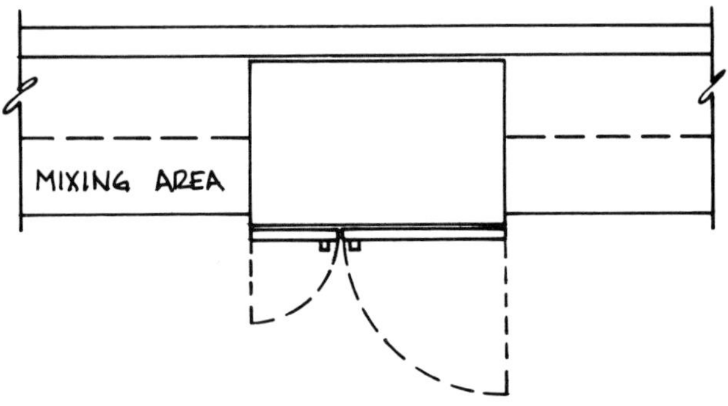

Figure 12. Leave countertop space on both sides of a side-by-side refrigerator.

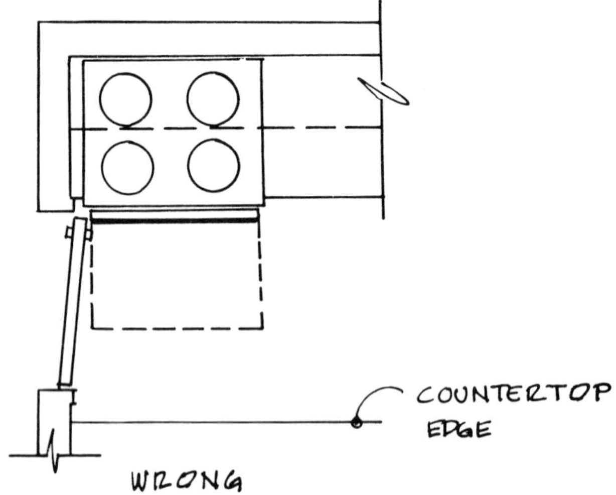

Figure 13. Place the range so that the oven door doesn't collide with the kitchen door.

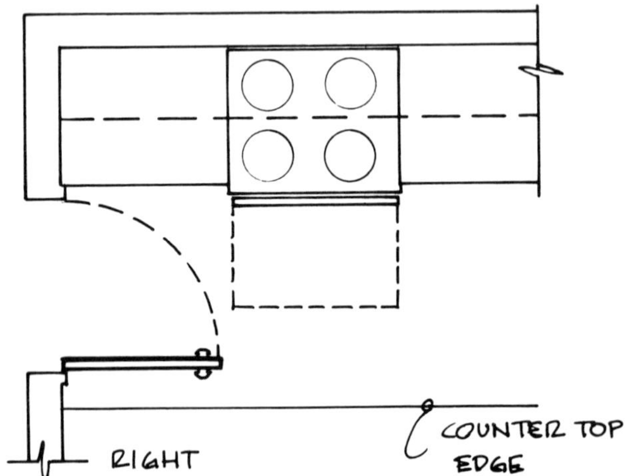

Figure 14. The kitchen door may open into the next room if it's not a hallway, or it may swing against the sides of the cabinets.

of space on each side for pot handles. (See Figure 16.)

Avoid placing the cook top or range under a window or in a drafty area. (See Figure 17.) Position gas stoves away from drafts because the pilot light and flames can be blown out. Placing any stove under a window is dangerous because curtains or window coverings can catch fire. Such positioning also prohibits the installation of hoods for ventilation and lighting. (Allow at least 15 inches of countertop from the range to the window.)

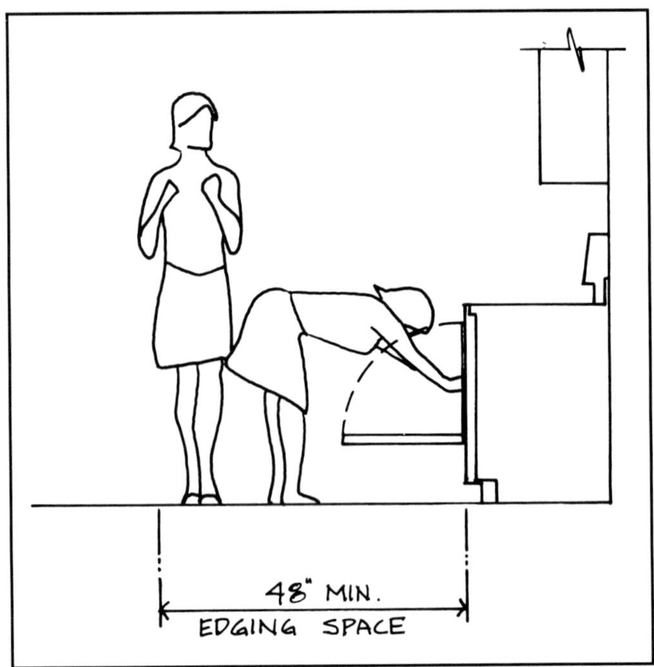

Figure 15. Placement of the oven should allow at least 48 inches of clearance for the door and edging space.

A liberal oven door clearance of 60 inches allows someone to walk by safely while the door is in use.

Microwaves are versatile and may be included in the range unit with either gas or electric ranges. They may be installed above the cook top or as part of a separate wall-oven installation. They are best installed as part of the mixing center, rather than the cooking

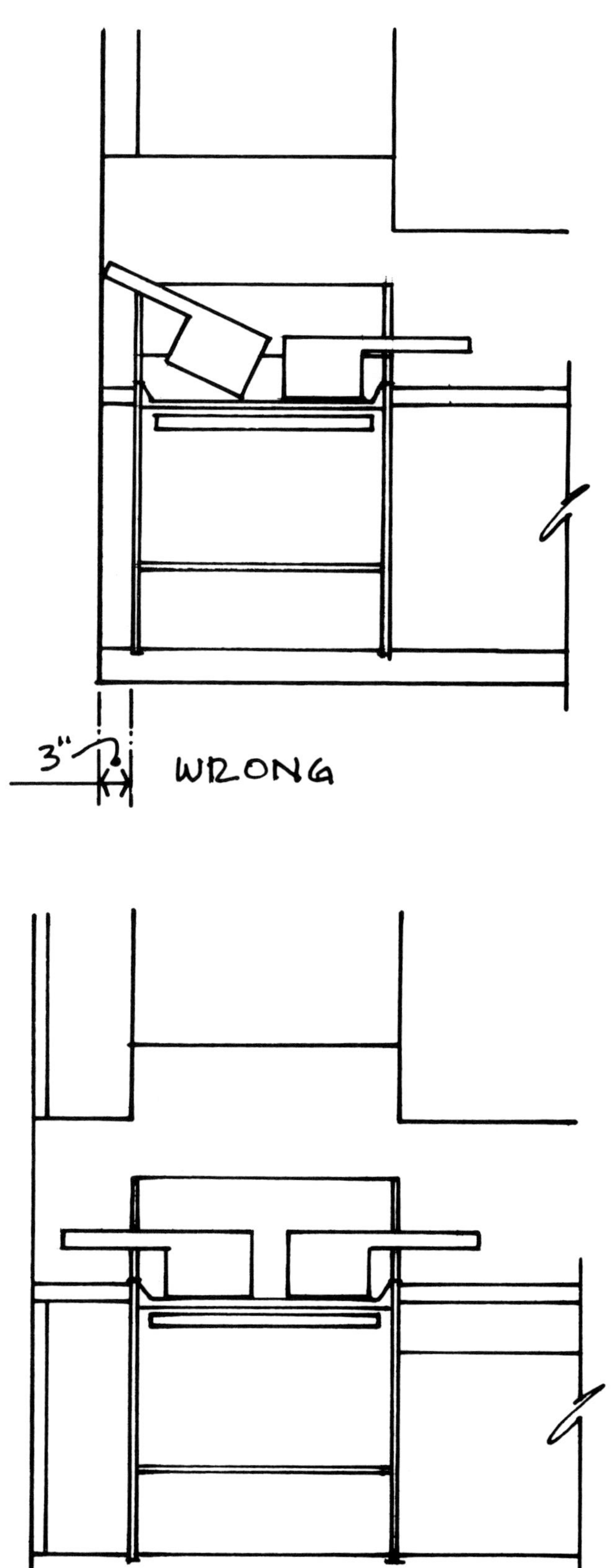

Figure 16. Allow 12 to 15 inches (from edge of the burners) of space on each side for pot handles.

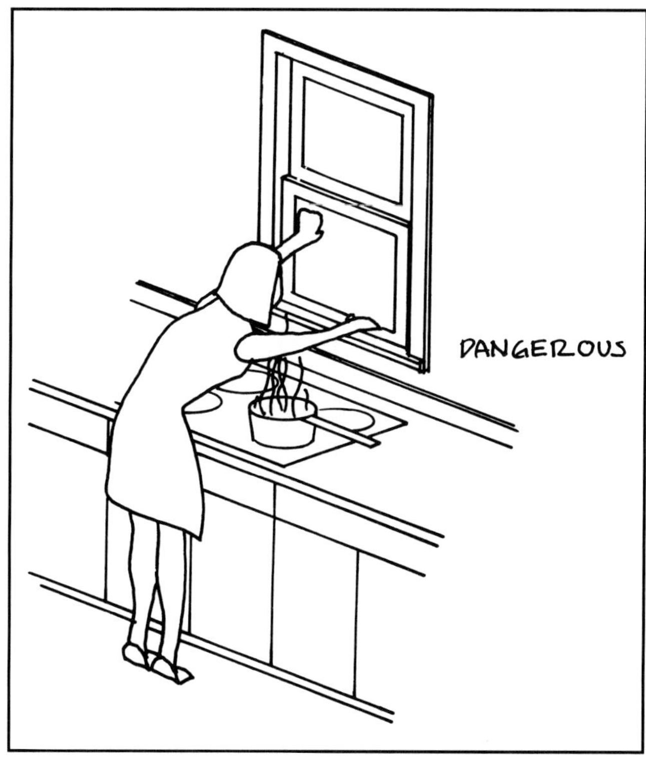

Figure 17. Avoid placing the range or cook top under a window. Allow 15 inches between the edge of the cooking unit and a window.

center, since they are used mostly for heating frozen foods, warming foods, defrosting, and baking.

The latest development in ranges is the multimode oven. These are combination thermal-microwave or convection-microwave ovens that eliminate the need for two installations.

Islands must also have electrical circuits that should be placed on the side, not the top, to avoid damage from spills. The wiring must be installed through the floor.

Plan for and include a hood. Island cook tops must have hoods appropriate for the area. Venting to the exterior may be difficult for this type of installation and must be carefully planned ahead of time. Because of length and possible turns of ductwork for island cook tops, larger ducting may be necessary. Both standard cook tops and downdraft units require exterior ducting. Never put a barbecue on an island, no matter how well vented; drafts will send fumes and smoke throughout the house.

Most hoods are lighted, and the minimum wattage should be two 75-watt bulbs or one 36-inch, 20-watt fluorescent light. Hoods should include fans as well as lights. (See Chapters 6 and 7 for more information on lighting and ventilation.)

The range center should include room for the following:

- Pots, pans, and lids
- Utensils
- Electrical equipment, such as corn poppers toasters, coffee makers, griddles
- Storage for pastas, tea, coffee, uncooked

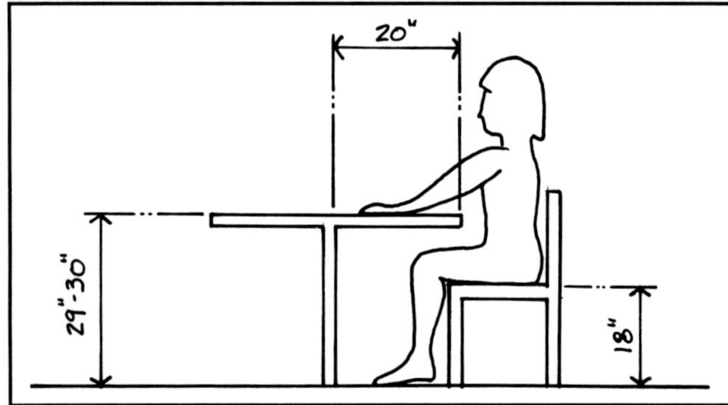

Figure 18. A table-height counter is 29 to 30 inches high and requires 20 inches of overhang for knee room.

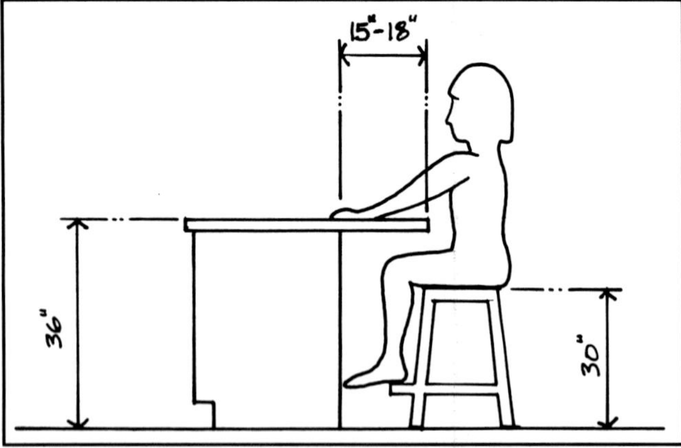

Figure 19. A standard counter requires 15 to 18 inches of overhang.

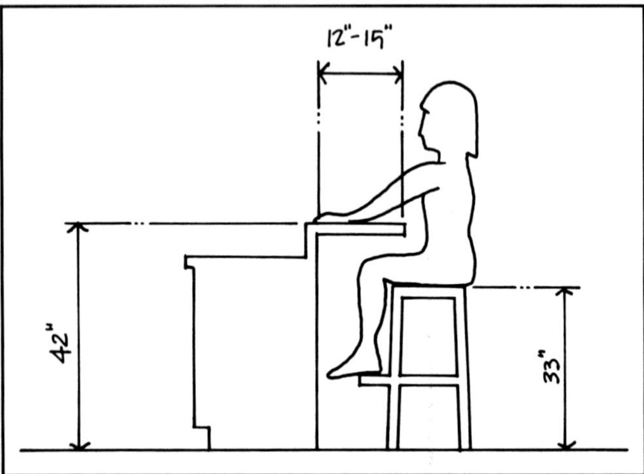

Figure 20. A bar-height counter requires 12 to 15 inches of overhang.

cereals, and any items that require cooking with water or milk

The mixing center, first of the secondary work centers, is an essential part of a well-organized kitchen. Place the mixing center between the refrigerator and the clean-up center. This allows easy access to ingredients and easy washing of fruits and vegetables prior to preparation.

This center should provide space for the following:

- Mixing bowls
- Utensils
- Measuring bowls
- Electrical equipment, such as mixers, blenders, food processors, and can openers
- Casseroles and baking pans
- Storage for canned goods, spices, flour, and sugar

Next to the mixing center, place the serving center. It may be a minimum of 15 inches alongside the cook top/range or a more generous area that allows space for platters, serving dishes, or even a buffet set-up.

For serving convenience, place the eating center near the cook top or range. Position it away from the work triangle and from the traffic flow within the kitchen.

In smaller kitchens, finding the space for an eating center is often a problem, but imaginative use of space can be the answer. A number of options exist, such as opening up a wall and creating a counter used both in the kitchen and in the family area. Extending a counter either through a curve or angled peninsula also solves the problem.

In larger kitchens, an informal counter arrangement is possible, perhaps using part of an island, along with a table arrangement, or a banquette. Basic rules must be observed, however. A space that looks large on a plan may not be large enough for a table for four; or the counter may need extra inches to seat two people comfortably.

Seating areas in the kitchen are generally for family use and need not be expandable to accommodate guests. Table space for four or counter space for two to four people is usually sufficient. In small units, table space for two suffices.

The *Kitchen Industry Technical Manual of 1984*, published by the National Kitchen and Bath Association and compiled by the Small Homes Council - Building Research Council, uses the following guidelines for determining eating space requirements.

Each seating place requires at least 24 inches for elbow room. This space permits the use of armless chairs or stools. If armchairs are to be used, allow 26 inches. Thus, a counter for four with armless stools must be 96 inches long.

A table-height counter should be 29 to 30 inches high and requires 20 inches of overhang for knee space. Chairs should be 18 inches high. A standard counter height of 36 inches requires a 15- to 18-inch overhang and a stool 24 to 25 inches high. A bar-height counter (42 inches) requires 12 to 15 inches of overhang. (See Figures 18, 19, and 20.)

The clearance for pulling counter chairs or stools out from under tables is at least 26 inches, the same as that for table chairs. But 36 inches is preferable (See Figure 21). A liberal space of 44 inches allows enough room for a walkway. Add another 2 inches to allow for door swing, if needed.

The clearance for pulling counter chairs or stools out from under tables is at least 26 inches, the same as that for table chairs. But 36 inches is preferable. (See Figure 21.) A liberal space of 44 inches allows enough room for a walkway. Add another 2 inches to allow for door swing, if needed.

A table also requires a minimum of 24 inches of space per person. The smallest table that seats six people, two on each side and one on each end, is 36 X 60 inches. (See Figure 22.) A round table 48 inches in diameter also seats six.

A banquette saves some space because it is immobile. A booth arrangement also takes less space.

A table should be placed 50 inches from a counter or 58 inches from an appliance, such as the range, when the table is in the kitchen. This allows a person enough room to work in the kitchen while the table is occupied. If the table is outside the working area, then the usual clearances apply.

Once you have planned the eating center, consider the planning and entertainment centers. No specific criteria govern the design for these centers. If you're including a planning center, place it outside the work triangle and provide sufficient light and space to permit a chair to be pushed back and an adequate passageway behind.

The Four Basic Kitchen Layouts

Over the past years, home economists, designers, architects, and manufacturers have analyzed the kitchen's use. The number of steps necessary to prepare a meal, to put away groceries, to clean and store vegetables—all the functions performed in the kitchen—were subjected to a series of studies. These studies produced the most desirable kitchen layouts, using the work triangle as the basis.

Experts now generally agree that the best designs derive from four basic layouts: the U-shape, the L-shape, the two-wall or corridor kitchen, and the one-wall kitchen.

The usual square space allocated for the kitchen in floor plans is adapted easily to both the U and the L layouts, either of which should be the first choice for builders.

Possibilities for creating an efficient design abound. At the planning stage, shifting a wall or removing it entirely to replace it with a counter, extending a cabinet run to form a peninsula, adding an island, changing the placement of a door or window, or creating a new window configuration are changes that make a world of difference in the long run and cost little or nothing if they are part of the original plan.

A careful study of these layouts shows ideal arrangements of the work centers in each to form desirable work triangles. The layouts can be adapted to various room sizes and changed to add more appliances or amenities.

U-shape

The U-Shape is the most desirable because it removes the working part of the kitchen from the remainder of the There is no danger of the kitchen becoming a traffic

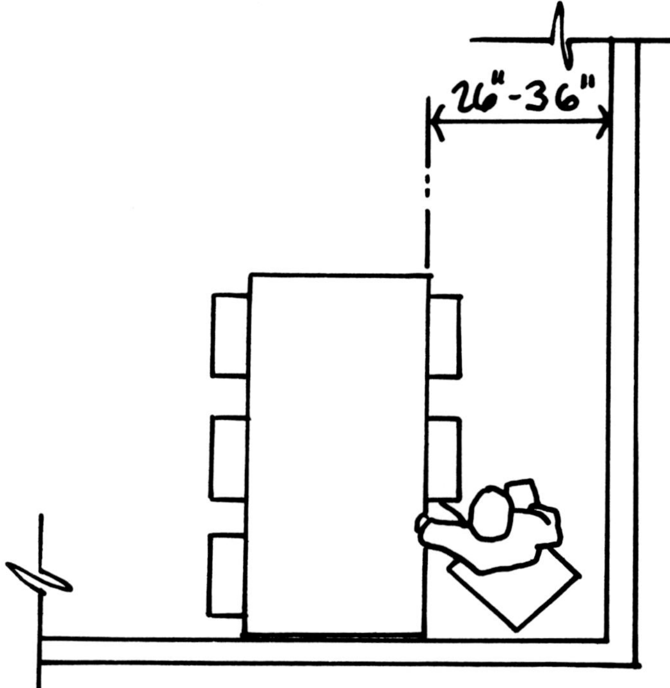

Figure 21. Chairs or stools at a table or counter require at least 26 inches of space for clearance; a clearance of 36 inches is better.

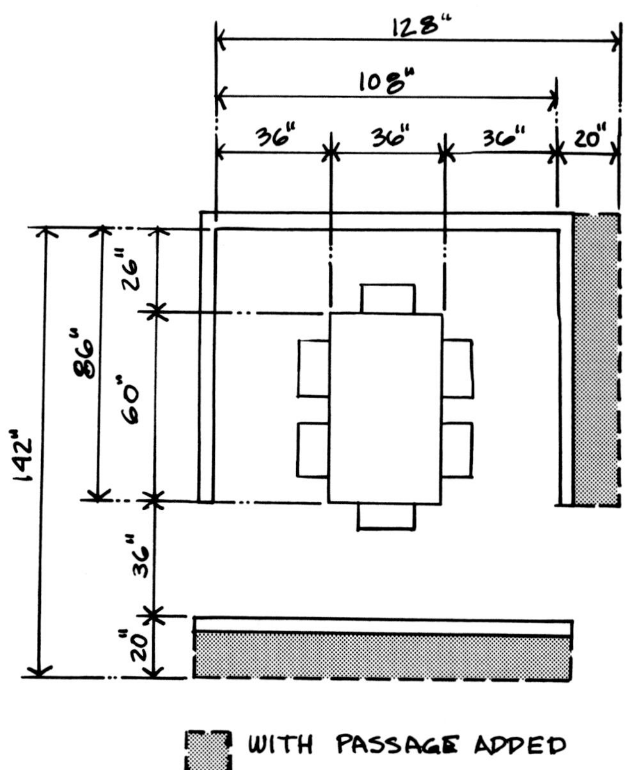

Figure 22. Minimum table size to seat six is 36 X 60 inches. Clearance for chairs and passageways are indicated.

corridor: access doors are outside the work triangle.

The U-shape easily accommodates a compact, efficient triangle. A logical location for the clean-up center is in the center of the U—an obvious place for a window as well.

The U-shape adapts simply to variations. In a large

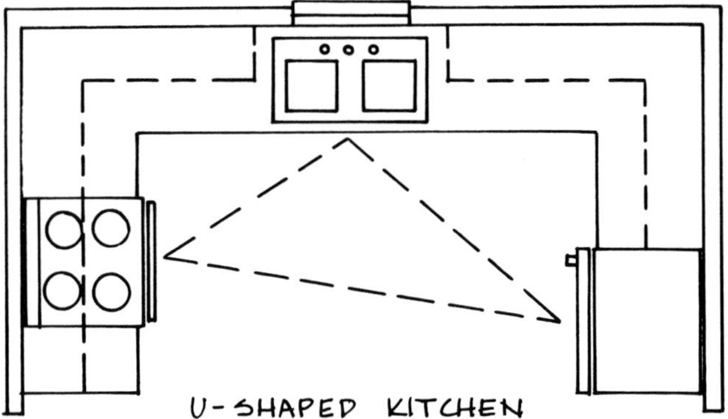

Figure 23. This layout removes the kitchen from the traffic pattern of the house. Considered to be the most efficient design, it is compact, easy to remove from the rest of the house, or to incorporate into a more open space.

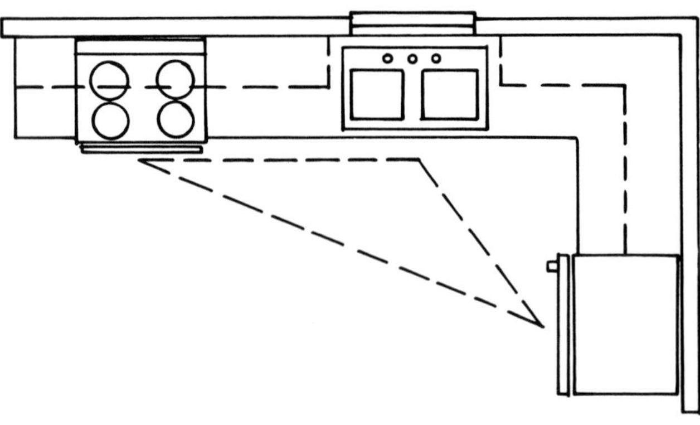

L-SHAPED KITCHEN

Figure 24. This layout generally fits easily into most floor plans. It protects the kitchen from use as a thoroughfare and lends itself to open plans and eat-in styles. It can also be separated from living quarters.

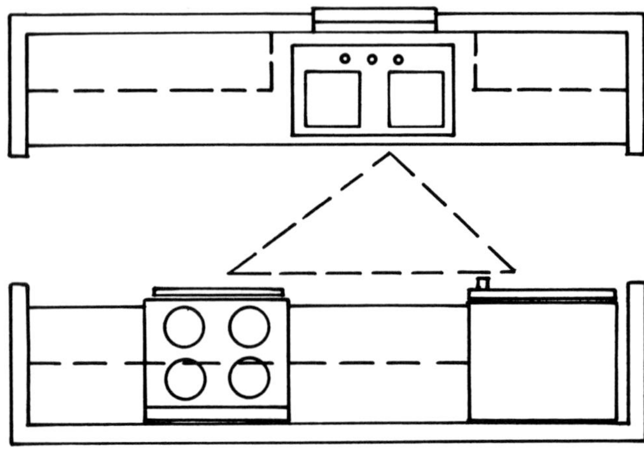

CORRIDOR KITCHEN
(TWO-WALL)

Figure 25. This layout allows for a good work triangle. It should have only one access door and requires at least 8 feet of width to permit the opening of appliance doors.

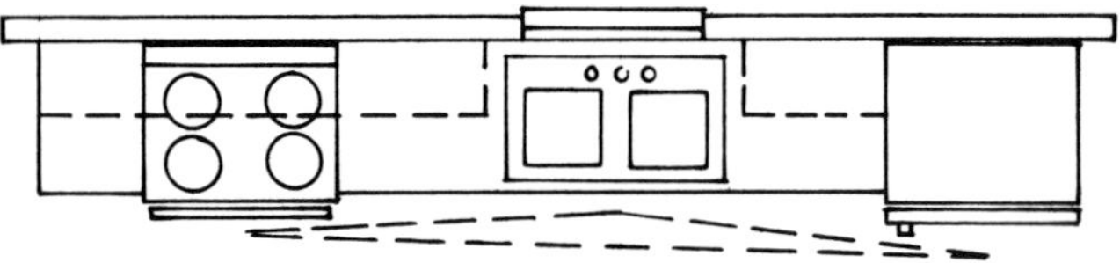

ONE-WALL KITCHEN

Figure 26. This is the least desirable layout, although it may be the only option for smaller units. Note the lengthy work triangle. Changing the wall facing the appliances into an island or counter creates a more efficient and attractive design. Then the island can be used for the sink or the cook top, with storage underneath for trays, large pots, or serving pieces.

enough room, add an island in the center of the open end for eating or kitchen tasks. One arm of the U may also be angled into a peninsula. A secondary access door may be added in one arm of the U.

L-shape

The L-shape is also highly desirable because it fits naturally into most floor plans and lends itself to an efficient work triangle. It excludes through-traffic and adapts to the open feeling that consumers prefer. (See Figure 24.)

Add a peninsula or an island to the L to create handsome variations that enhance the usefulness of the room. These can be eating centers, supplemen-tary cooking or clean-up centers, or combinations of these. The L may be broken at its juncture in another variation.

Two-Wall

The two-wall or corridor kitchen (Figure 25) is a narrow room witht he appliances placed on opposite walls. The walk space in the corridor must be a minimum of 48 inches wide to permit the opening of the appliance doors and the passage of two people. This minimum passageway requires a room that is 96 inches wide. (Base appliances are 24 inches deep and require 48 inches for door openings.)

At this size only one person at a time can use this room comfortably. Build only one access door to the corridor because traffic through the kitchen is annoying and dangerous.

To accommodate two people comfortably, leave 60 inches for passageway space, which makes the corridor 108 inches wide.

One-Wall

As the name implies, the one-wall kitchen is a room with all the appliances lined up along one wall (Figure 26). It can be varied by eliminating the wall opposite the appliances and creating an open room. A counter or island instead of the wall serves as a room divider and helps create a sense of greater space.

The one-wall kitchen is used in designs that combine the living and working space (as described above) or when there is limited space. It is generally less efficient because the work triangle must be extended. Placing the cook top on an island increases efficiency.

Design this kitchen with one access door, if possible, and in a minimum of 96 inches of width to permit opening of appliance doors.

Chapter 4
Cabinets

The talents of kitchen designers have been put to good use in today's market. Kitchen cabinets come in a spectacular range of styles that enable the builder to satisfy a wide spectrum of tastes.

While the majority of buyers still want wooden cabinets, interest in European-style laminates is increasing, particularly among urban, upscale consumers.

Consumers overwhelmingly prefer medium-toned woods, according to one survey, which revealed that 62 percent of respondents favored them, while 24 percent preferred light woods; and 15 percent preferred dark woods. Interest in white kitchens is increasing (*Kitchen and Bath Business* 1984).

As far as cabinet style goes, 34 percent of those surveyed chose cathedral doors, followed in popularity by the raised-panel door, chosen by 29 percent; 24 percent preferred a flat door (*Kitchen and Bath Business* 1984).

The most important aspect of cabinet design is how cabinets are arranged and what they must include. The usual dead space in kitchens can be imaginatively used to provide the home owner with additional storage and utility amenities.

Imaginative uses of space contribute to the sales appeal of the house. Consider the difference between standard kitchen cabinets and those with pull-out waste baskets, tilt-out drawers under the sink for storage, lazy susan corner cabinets, and attractive open shelves for display. In both eye appeal and convenience, the latter far surpasses the former.

Performance Standards

Prior to World War II, kitchen cabinets were usually custom made, and many were designed and built by the carpenter on the job site. These cabinets were metal, and stock wooden ones as we know them today were unavailable.

Satisfying the enormous demand created by the post-war housing boom was beyond the capacity of the small custom shop or the carpenter. So mass production of kitchen cabinets was born, and with it, new concepts in convenience and good looks.

As in many industries, a need to establish quality standards in kitchen construction arose to protect the consumer and the builder. In response to this need, the American National Standards Institute (ANSI) set standards that are recognized by the National Kitchen Cabinet Association (NKCA).

These standards govern the construction and performance of the cabinets and cover operation of overloaded drawers and shelves, resistance to abuse, such as that inflicted by children, and the ability to withstand extreme temperature changes, humidity, and such substances as detergents, vinegar, alcohol, and olive oil.

Cabinet manufacturers submit their cabinets to the American Council of Independent Laboratories for testing to receive the certification seal of the NKCA. Membership in NKCA is not mandatory for certification.

ANSI standards are recognized as those minimally acceptable by the U.S. Department of Housing and Urban Development (HUD), the U.S. League of Savings and Loans, and the American Institute of Kitchen Dealers. These are a builder's assurance that the cabinetry will perform as advertised.

Stock and Custom Cabinets

Although kitchen cabinets can still be built on the job, the majority are either stock or custom cabinets.

Stock cabinets are built to standard specifications in the factory and warehoused until ordered. Stock manufacture allows for quality control and precise measurements.

Stock cabinet manufacturers are no longer confining themselves, however, to a few basic styles. Builders can match cabinets with valences and other trims,

Courtesy Wood-Mode Cabinetry

Figure 27. Innovative cabinetry has enormous appeal.

including hood cabinets, handsome open shelves, wine racks, and appliance panels, all extras that add sales appeal.

Custom-built cabinets are designed and built to individual specifications. The height, width, and depth can be varied to fit the job, and special features can be added that are unavailable in a stock cabinet. In addition, various units, such as built-in desks, even gun cases, can be ordered. Paneling and wainscoting, as well as other accents, are available to match the cabinets. Today, the kitchen cabinet manufacturer is making furniture that can easily be used in other parts of the home. Detail and variety of materials offer the builder a dazzling array of choices.

Choosing stock or custom cabinetry depends on the price of the home. Whichever you choose, the quality should be the best possible. The consumer ranks quality as the top priority in selecting cabinets.

Often the dollars spent to upgrade the kitchen cabinets means a sizeable increase in a home's selling price. Offering upgraded cabinetry as an option helps realize higher profits, since profit margin on the cabinetry is not included in the price of the home.

Making the Floor Plan

Appliance size dictates the use of space in the kitchen and the size of the cabinets.

To help you plan a kitchen, this chapter describes the amount of base cabinet, wall cabinet, and countertop surface recommended, the countertop surface required for each work center and activity, the amount of clearance needed between cabinets and appliances, a guide to vertical placement, and a comprehensive sample floor plan. In Appendix 1 you will find templates representing standard-sized appliances, a chart of drafting symbols, patterns for typical wall and base cabinets, and graph paper for making a floor plan.

Photocopy the graph paper and templates, so they can be reused. Cut out the templates of the appliances and cabinets you plan to use. Cabinet manufacturers furnish dimension charts. If you plan to use appliances other than standard ones, get the dimensions from the manufacturer or your appliance dealer.

Courtesy Wood-Mode Cabinetry

Figure 28. Cathedral and glass-front cabinets complement this country kitchen.

The *Kitchen Industry Technical Manual of 1984* established minimum and liberal frontage measurements for base cabinets, wall cabinets, and countertop surfaces, clearances needed for proper meal preparation and other activities, and dimensions of work centers.

Minimum clearances and frontages are for housing units of up to 1,000 square feet. Liberal clearances and frontages are for units of 1,400 square feet or more. Intermediate-sized units should have clearances and frontages that border on the liberal. When designing large kitchens, remember that bigger is not necessarily better: keep the work triangle 22 feet or less, if possible. In small apartments it may be impossible to meet recommended minimums.

The established minimum base cabinet frontage is 72 inches, measured along the front edge of the cabinets. The liberal frontage is 120 inches. In the work center, do not exceed 180 inches, as the distances among work centers will be too great. Exclude appliances from the cabinet frontage measurement.

Base cabinets should have at least nine drawers or pull-out shelves. One drawer should be deep and wide (12 inches X 24 inches), and one should be shallow, for tableware.

Wall cabinets are designed to provide storage for china and serving pieces, among other items. Recommended frontage is based on dinnerware requirements. The minimum for a service for four is 72 inches; the liberal measurement is 120 inches. For a service for 12, the minimum frontage is 120 inches, and the liberal frontage is 168 inches.

Wall cabinets should be hung over counters. At least 42 inches of wall cabinet frontage should be placed within 72 inches of the sink for handy storage of dishware.

Countertop surfaces are measured along the front edge of the counters. (Sink and cook top surfaces are excluded from the total.) The recommended countertop measurements appear in Table 2.

Table 2

Recommended Countertop Measurements for Work Centers

Work Center	*Recommended Measurement (inches)*	*Minimum Measurement (inches)*
Mixing center	42	36
Clean-up center		
one side	36	24
other side	30	18
Range/cook top		
one side	24	15
other side	18	12
Separate built-in oven	18	15
Refrigerator opening side	18	15

When one counter is used for more than one function, the countertop surface should be the length of the longest counter plus 12 inches. For instance, if the sink, mixing center, and refrigerator share a counter, the length of that counter should equal the length of the mixing center, 42 inches, plus 12 inches—or 54 inches.

It is essential to provide adequate room between counters and appliances to prepare meals, serve, eat, and clean up. A liberal clearance allows room for one person to walk past another who is using an appliance or cabinet. Minimum clearances allow edging space. (See Table 3.)

Table 3 - Recommended Working Clearances

Location	*Minimum (inches)*	*Liberal (inches)*
Between base cabinets or appliances opposite each other	48	60
Between base cabinets or appliances at right angles to each other	30	38
Between base cabinet front and table, wall, or storage wall	48	60
Between storage wall front and table or wall		
with passageway	30	44
without passageway	30*	38*
Between table and wall or base cabinet side or back		
with passageway	30	44
without passageway	26	36

* *This measurement assumes the use of sliding doors. For storage walls with hinged or folding doors, allow space for the door to swing plus 16 inches or the clearance listed above, whichever is greater.*

Using the appliance dimensions in Appendix 1 as a guide, lay the templates on the graph to indicate the position of each appliance, creating a work triangle no more than 22 feet nor less than 12 feet. Position the sink between the range and the refrigerator.

The sample floor plan is a kitchen with many extras, such as a planning desk, to show a complex layout. (See Figure 29.) Note the compact work triangle in this large area. Warming drawers are included close to the entrance to the dining room. A baking center and bar area are next to the family room. (This arrangement is ideal for empty-nesters who like to entertain.)

After arranging the appliances, sketch in the cabinet layout. Consider making changes in wall placement, windows, and doors. You may want to relocate the kitchen to improve its relationship to the garage and the play areas. Use ingenious ways to devise sufficient work and storage space, such as installing a pull-out or fold-up table or sliding wall units.

After sketching in the desired layout, check measurements carefully using inches, not feet. If a wall measurement is 100 inches from stud to stud, allow for sheetrock installation to determine the actual measurement. Take the measurement of each component and add them together; then check against overall measurements. After the studs are erected, check measurements again.

Typical Appliance Dimensions and Counter Requirements

Standard sinks are 21 inches from front to back, including the lip for faucet installation. Single bowls measure 24 to 30 inches across, double bowls, 32 to 42 inches across, and triple bowls, 45 to 48 inches.

Allow a minimum of 18 inches of counter space on one side of the sink and 24 inches on the other. Liberal allowances are 30 and 36 inches.

Standard ranges/cook tops and multimode ovens are 20 to 48 inches wide; 30 inches is the most popular size. Commercial stoves are wider.

Allow a minimum of 15 inches for countertops on each side of the range or cook top. A better allowance is 24 inches on one side and 15 inches on the other.

Wall-ovens are built to fit into 24- to 30-inch cabinets. Allow a minimum of 15 inches of heatproof counter on one side. A better allowance is 24 inches, with additional space on the other side.

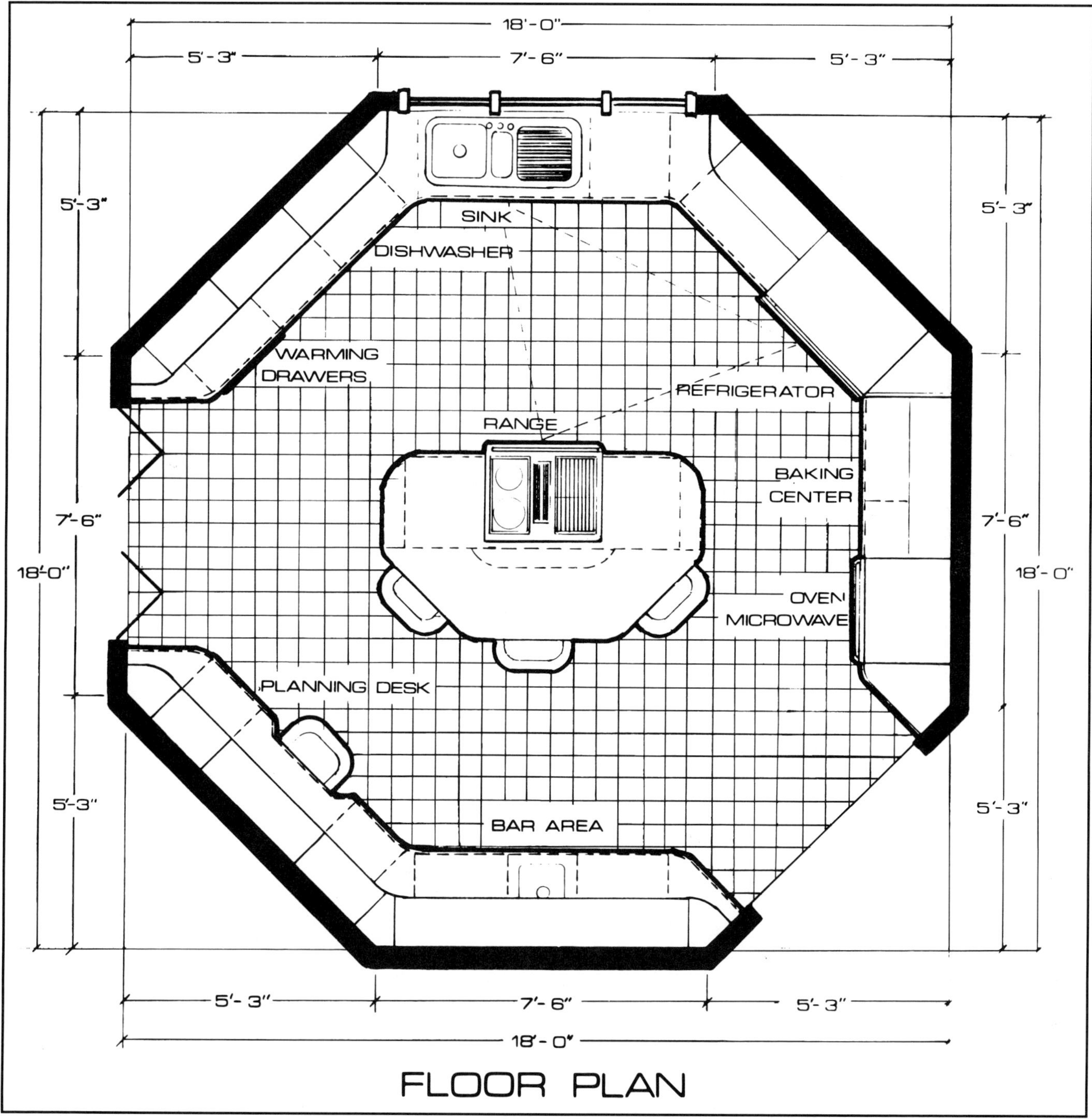

Courtesy Dean Ingram, CKD, and Maytag Company

Figure 29. A comprehensive floor plan with many extras

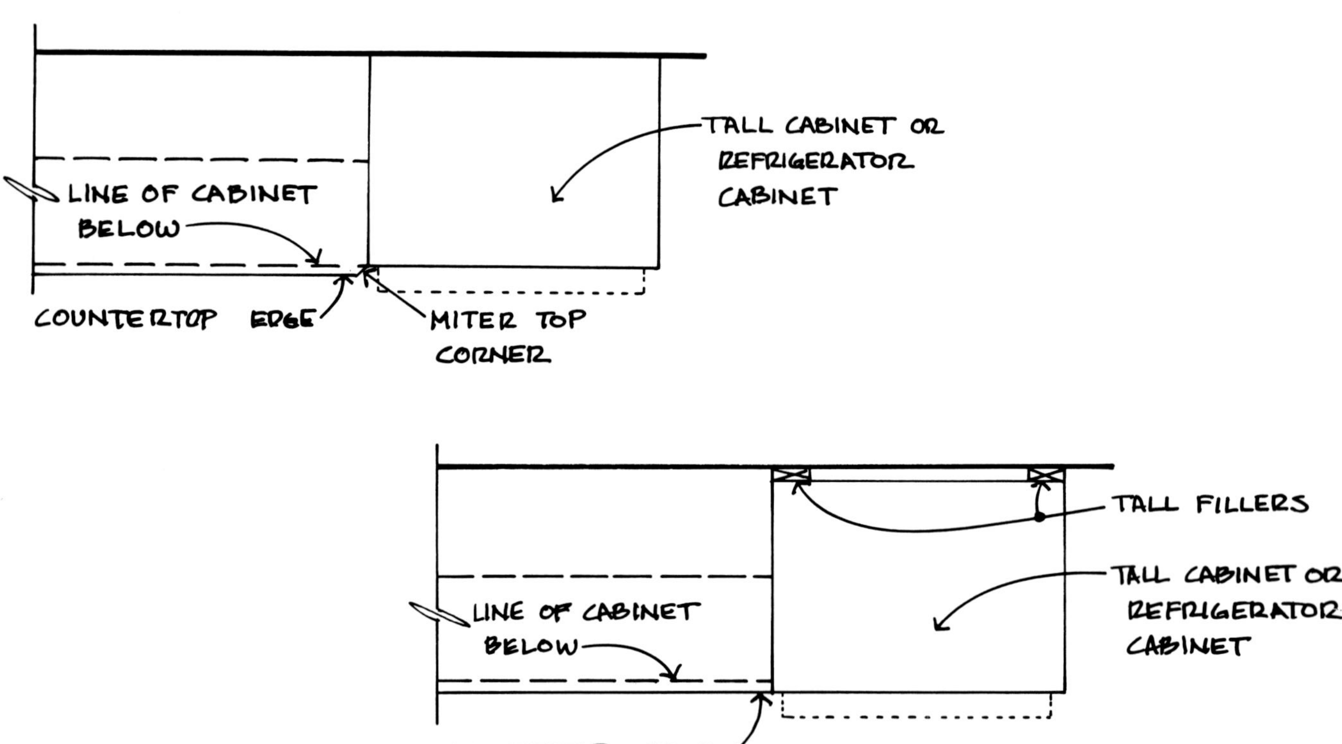

Figure 30. Two methods of aligning the counter with the refrigerator

Microwave ovens are from 24 to 33 inches wide. Provide 24 to 26 inches of counter space adjacent to the microwave.

Refrigerators are 30 to 42 inches wide, the only appliances that do not fit into the standard 24-inch-deep cabinet. Big, bulky, and protruding, the refrigerator presents a problem.

Several solutions are available. Surround the refrigerator with cabinets placed flush with its front, and the front can be paneled to match. These cabinets can provide pantry space or a broom/vacuum or ironing center. This arrangement, however, does not provide counter space for getting food out of the refrigerator or for storing groceries. Ample counter space must be available to facilitate refrigerator use.

Another solution is to flush out a cabinet on one side only, providing a pantry, and then building the standard 24-inch-deep counter on the other so it's flush with the side of the refrigerator. Or miter the countertop to fit. (See Figure 30.)

Side-by-side refrigerators run 30 to 42 inches in width. They must be installed with enough space for both doors to open to full stops. Doors generally need more than a 90-degree opening for proper use. Side-by-sides are designed for installation in a right-hand position at the right end of the work area. They require a work counter on both sides, if possible.

Single-door refrigerators are also 30 to 42 inches wide. Right-hand doors should be at the right end of the counter run, and the door should open away from the counter to be used for mixing. If designing a kitchen for a left-handed person, reverse the order.

Water connections must be installed for icemaker models. Roll-out models are more convenient and easier to maintain. A minimum side clearance of 2-½ inches must be allowed on the return wall.

A 1-inch ventilation space must be allowed at the top. Most refrigerators have a 2-inch leveling adjustment.

Standard refrigerators range from 10 cubic feet to 27 cubic feet. (Refer to the templates for installation space required.) Refrigerators must have a minimum of 6 inches of clearance between the appliance and an end wall to allow the door to open past 90 degrees. Refrigerators are usually 58 to 72 inches high.

If you are considering installing a built-in refrigerator, such as the Sub-Zero, you must use special plans and cabinetry. Sub-Zeros are 24 inches from front to back and have compressors on top.

Allow 36 to 42 inches of counter space between the refrigerator and sink for the mixing center.

An additional refrigerator in a bar or entertainment area is a welcome convenience in the luxury market. New refrigerators have expanded space that accommodates six-packs and three-liter bottles. They can be installed under the counter or set in at eye level, as part of the above-counter cabinetry. Plans for installation must include electrical supply.

The dishwasher is an important appliance in today's kitchen. With 78 percent of the consumers stating that they wanted dishwashers, builders offer them 92 percent of the time (*Professional Builder* 1985).

Typical units fit under a standard 36-inch-high, 24-inch (front-to-back counter. For smaller kitchens, 18-

inch-wide dishwashers are available.

The undersink dishwasher is a welcome addition to the small kitchen and uses often wasted undercounter space. These are 24 inches wide and require special compatible sinks. Sinks are offered in two styles: a 6-inch-deep single bowl, which fits a 24-inch counter space, and a 6-inch-deep double bowl, which fits a 36-inch counter space and has a full under sink or an offset installation. The offset installation allows the 12 inches necessary for a disposal.

Dishwashers are now available with black glass fronts, as well as custom front panels of wood and laminates.

Electronically controlled dishwashers have touch pad controls and micro-processors that automatically monitor the machine's performance and provide alert signals during a malfunction.

Clothes washers and dryers are not usually a part of the kitchen. In some house plans, however, such placement is desirable, and in smaller homes, apartments, and condominiums, the stacked washer/dryer is often installed in the kitchen.

Standard measurements for side-by-side washers and dryers are 60 inches wide by 27 inches high by 30 inches deep. These do not fit into standard cabinets. Doors are usually used to conceal the appliances, and shelf units may be provided above them.

Standard Cabinet Measurements

The size of cabinets has been standardized, which simplifies matters. Both stock and custom manufacturers use the same basic dimensions. Manufacturers, however, may offer a different range of sizes. Each manufacturer has specification sheets for his products, which give the configuration and the dimensions of the cabinets offered.

The standard height for base cabinets is 36 inches. (In custom homes customers may prefer a 37-½-inch height.) This dimension comprises the cabinet, 30-½ inches, toe space and base, 4 inches, and countertop, 1-½ inches. The overall height can be raised by adding an extra inch to the countertop, changing base heights, or adding shallow drawers under the top. The standard depth is 24 inches from front to back. Linear footage varies. Base cabinets increase in 3-inch and 6-inch increments and may start as small as 9 inches and go up to 84 inches.

Base cabinets are available for sinks or cooktops, peninsulas, corners, in angled cabinet shapes, in end corners, with lazy susans, for sewing machines, with fold-out tables, and with special drawer arrangements for everything from canned goods to waste baskets.

Lazy susans or drum carousels are usually available in 33-inch and 36-inch dimensions. Dead corner turnouts are generally 48 inches.

In laying out base cabinets, allow for recommended working clearances. Between appliances and other counters, 48 inches is the minimum space for clearance.

Wall cabinets are 12 to 13 inches from front to back, although some manufacturers offer them in 24-inch depths. Heights and widths vary, with 12- to 48-inch heights and widths available in some large lines. When hung over a base cabinet, they should be 15 to 18 inches above the base cabinet to allow space for small appliances.

The wall cabinet's top shelf should be no more than 72 inches from the floor, or it is too high for the average person. Adjustable shelves solve this problem.

Double access cabinets are also available, useful for hanging over peninsula counters. Cabinets hung over peninsulas or islands should be 25 inches above the countertop and set back at least 3 inches from the edge of the base.

Base cabinets should have a minimum of nine drawers or pull-out shelves. One drawer should be deep and wide (12 inches X 24 inches), and one should be shallow, for tableware.

Wall cabinets are designed to provide storage for china and serving pieces, among other things. Recommended frontage for these, based on dinnerware service requirements, is as follows:

Frontage	*Service for 4*	*Service for 12*
Minimum	72 inches	120 inches
Medium	96 inches	144 inches
Liberal	120 inches	168 inches

Cabinets hung over refrigerators present special problems. If the refrigerator is installed in a flushed-out wall, the space above the appliance can be used for part of the cabinet run. If the refrigerator is quite tall, the space may be almost inaccessible without a ladder. One solution is to simply fill the space with false fronts. Another is to frame around the top, leaving a 10- or 12-inch-deep recess for open shelves.

Cabinets over refrigerators, ranges, cook tops, and sinks should not be counted in these frontages, because the space is usually obstructed in some way by ducts, hoods, or inaccessibility.

In addition to linear measurements, consider vertical distribution of cabinets. (Refer to Figure 31.)

Some innovations in cabinetry that help sell homes are as follows:

- Packaged goods storage cabinets
- Chef's pantries
- Pull-out counters (especially for small kitchens)
- Mixer cabinets
- Waste receptacles
- Pull-out chopping blocks
- Sliding trays
- Wine racks
- Pantries
- Sewing machine cabinets
- Desks
- Broom/vacuum cabinets

Now that you've learned how to design an efficient kitchen, the next chapter, on appliances, countertops, and floors, explains how to enhance a kitchen's appeal.

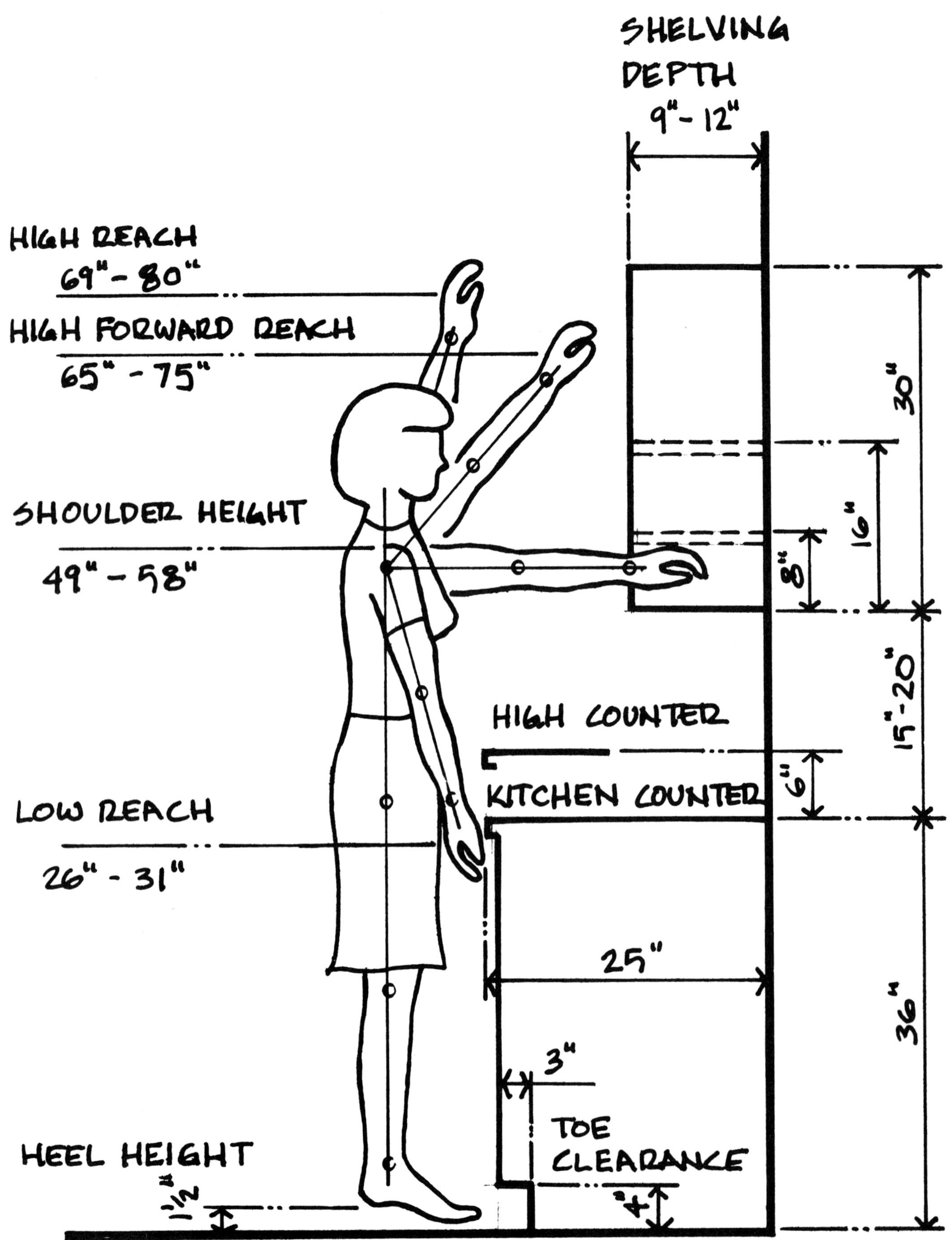

Figure 31. Vertical distribution

Chapter 5
Appliances, Countertops, and Floors

What's New?

In addition to the usual kitchen appliances, countertops, and floors, technology has created new features that characterize today's kitchen, adding convenience and efficiency. Built-ins are increasingly popular, as are electronic controls, particularly in luxury kitchens.

Built-ins offer a unified, smoothly coordinated look—very marketable—that's achieved by using panel doors matching the cabinetry that fit over refrigerator, compactor, and dishwasher doors.

All categories of major appliances now feature electronically controlled units. What are the advantages of electronic controls, and how can they help sell homes?

A smooth, clean, high-tech look is in style for kitchens, and electronic controls blend perfectly to enhance the overall effect. Their good looks also enhance traditional kitchens. In addition, electronic controls appeal to home owners because of easy maintenance: surfaces are smooth and do not collect grease and dirt. Electronic controls are "smart." The user can give the stove or other appliance instructions for several steps in a cycle. The appliance then automatically follows the sequence.

Furthermore, development of smart house systems (available by 1988 or 1989) will affect kitchens dramatically. The cabling and control system that interconnects all electrical, electronic, and gas-fired products in the home offers the following benefits for kitchen appliances:

- More safety
- Increased efficiency and economy
- Monitoring
- Remote control
- Appliance coordination
- Scheduled control
- Voice activation

Courtesy Whirlpool

Figure 32. Electronic controls are an innovation in kitchen appliances.

Many innovations appear in conventional appliances, as well. The following provides the latest information on kitchen appliances, countertops, and floors.

Cook Tops and Ovens

Solid element cook tops, an idea from Europe, offer the consumer a smooth, contemporary, high-tech look, with efficient cooking and easy maintenance. The cooking elements are cast iron, and contain electric resistance wires embedded in ceramic insulation. As the heat spreads through the element, it is conducted to the cookware. The element heats up gradually and retains heat. (See Figure 33.)

The microwave is so compact that it allows a kitchen designer a number of alternatives. A drop-in range with microwave is the immediate solution for kitchens

Courtesy Jenn-Air

Figure. 33 Solid element cook top

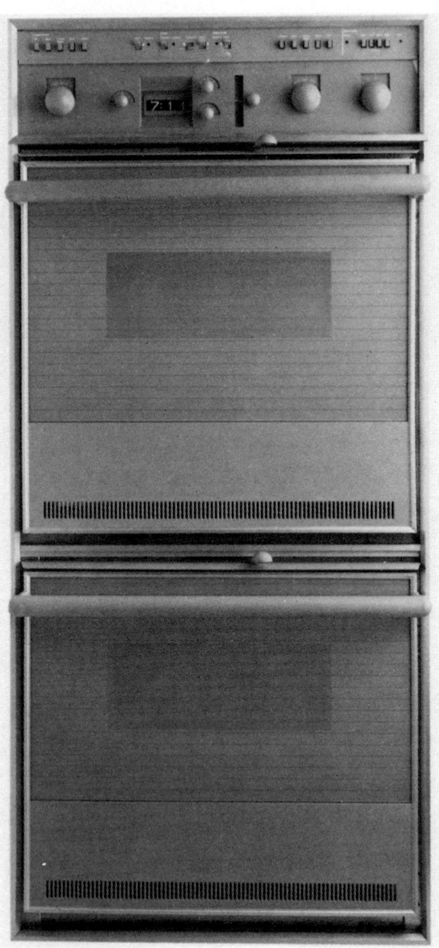

Courtesy Thermador

Figure 36. Multimode oven

Courtesy Hot Point

Figure 34. Drop-in range with microwave

Figure 35. Induction cook top

Courtesy General Electric

Courtesy General Electric

Figure 37. A microwave oven under a cabinet saves valuable counter space.

without built-in appliances. (See Figure 34.) Some include a hood and hood light, offering lighting, ventilation, and versatility. This set-up, however, requires reaching over the top of the burners to use the microwave, which may be hazardous, particularly for short people. Gas ranges now come with microwaves.

Induction cook tops have smooth, glass-like tops. They do not get hot and require little maintenance. They are the newest and most expensive cook tops, offering the speed of gas with the ability to control heat even at a very low temperature. Chocolate, for example, can be melted on these easily without burning.

An electromagnetic inducer creates a magnetic current that reacts with a magnetic metal pot or pan to transfer heat directly to the utensil and food. Since no elements are heated, no energy is wasted, and food cooks faster and more efficiently. Furthermore, there is no danger of being burned by touching a hot stove top or element. Only magnetic utensils such as steel, cast iron, and porcelain-enameled steel may be used on induction burners.

A multimode cook top, with interchangeable grills, deep-fat fryers, griddles, and wok accessories, is an excellent selling feature. You need not provide all interchangeable elements, but the home owner may purchase them as desired, and the versatility of the cook top is a selling point. These are available in conventional coil, glass-ceramic, induction, and solid element ranges. Multimode ovens microwave, bake, or do both simultaneously. Available in microwave-convection or microwave-thermal combinations, these are appropriate for the luxury market. (See Figure 36.)

The advent of the microwave oven revolutionized American cooking and eating habits. In one survey 43 percent of consumers listed microwaves as preference items as second ovens (National Association of Home Builders 1985). These appliances are selling points for any kitchen. (See Figure 37.) Considering the relatively inexpensive price, include microwaves as standard equipment in all but basic kitchens. In basic kitchens design space to accommodate a microwave, or install a combination range.

A separately installed microwave can be placed in the mixing center, close by the refrigerator, adjacent to the cook top, or near a bar and entertainment center, if it is close enough to the work triangle to be practical. Put the microwave in your initial plans. It requires cabinetry and electrical wiring that should be done at the rough-in stage.

Ideally, all microwaves that are not a part of the range should be installed so that the bottom shelf is elbow height plus or minus 6 inches from the floor. This height—from 36 inches to 48 inches from the floor—is convenient for a woman of average height (5 feet, 4 inches).

Allow a minimum of 24 inches of counter space under the microwave. If a separate microwave and oven are installed in the same wall, put a breadboard pull-out between them for convenience.

Doors to separate microwaves should open to the right for right-handed people, and counter space should be to the right. If it is necessary to use a left-opening door, allow for counter space to the left. The fold-down door can be used with counter space on either side or below.

The combination conventional oven and microwave is a built-in appliance that can be installed away from the cook top. More expensive, it is a sleek-looking, practical appliance for move-up and luxury kitchens.

Gas ranges continue to be a favorite with professionals and many gourmet cooks, as well as the average consumer. Now, gas ranges are available with pilotless ignition, a safety factor. An electrical hook-up is necessary for this feature.

Refrigerators

Manufacturers are designing more practical, more versatile, and now, more "intelligent" refrigerators—those with electronic controls.

Refrigerator choice depends on price, but the few hundred dollars' difference in a refrigerator with extras, such as electronic controls, makes an enormous difference to the home buyer. Automatic ice makers and cold water dispensers are not new but are highly desirable. Separate in-door compartments eliminate the need to open the full door and provide access to frequently used items. Refrigerators with refreshment centers are especially convenient for families with children: the centers provide shelves for preparing cold drinks and snacks. (See Figure 38.)

Courtesy Frigidaire

Figure 38. This side-by-side refrigerator has a refreshment center, convenient for families.

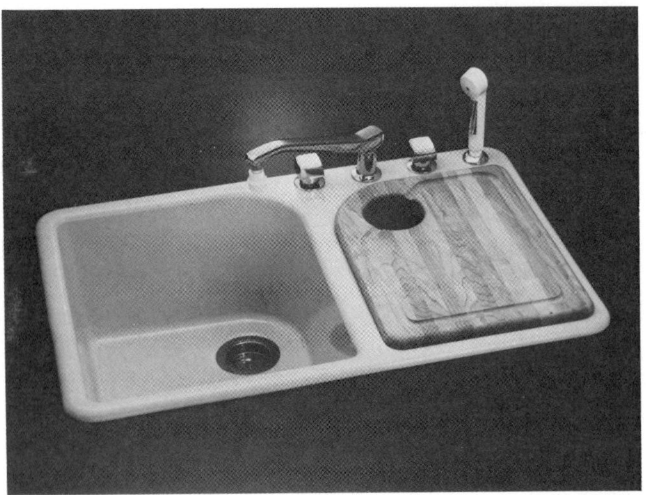

Courtesy Kohler

Figure 39. This double sink features an off-center drain, spayer, and cutting board.

Courtesy Moen

Figure 40. This riser faucet rises to over 10 inches above the sink for washing large pots, filling tall vases, and other household chores.

Sinks

In addition to the usual single or double sink, there are multiuse sinks. Double bowl sinks are preferred by 60 percent of purchasers, and 73 opted for stainless steel. Forty-six percent preferred a disposal. Among purchasers of more expensive kitchens, 20 percent added a hot water tap, and 73 percent installed a sprayer (*Kitchen and Bath Business* 1984).

Sinks are available that have many accessories. For example, offset drainholes offer more work room—the disposal does not usurp most of the undersink cabinet space. Sinks come with waste disposal chutes that empty into suspended trash cans, with removable drainboards, cutting boards, crockery baskets, colander half-sinks, and oversized bowls for oversized pots and pans. In addition, innovative features are available, such as electronic faucets that display water temperature; some faucets can be adjusted in height to facilitate filling gallon jugs or tall vases; a variety of new styles fit any decor.

Larger kitchens and those for specific markets, such as the empty nesters, should include an accessory sink in an entertainment area. This relieves the kitchen sink and provides an extra facility for clean-up after entertaining. Accessory sinks can also be placed in gardening rooms in custom-built homes.

Trash Compactors

The trash compactor is a specialty item, ideal for areas where trash disposal is difficult and for small spaces that can't accommodate large trash cans; it eliminates lugging trash to curbside.

If you include a trash compactor, place it in the sink area or in a utility area, removed from the food preparation area, where it does not occupy valuable under-counter space.

Disposals

The disposal is an inexpensive addition to the kitchen that should be standard at every market level except the basic, three-appliance kitchen or in areas where septic tanks are used. In the basic kitchen, add the disposal as a selling point. (Note that some areas prohibit disposals, and some areas require them.)

The disposal requires no extra pipes but does require wiring. The piping is incorporated into the sink piping, and the wiring is installed along with that of the dishwasher. For sales appeal, use an off-center drain sink to allow more under-counter space. This sets the pipes to the side and back, yet allows accessibility for disposal repairs.

Dishwashers

The dishwasher is a preference item with over 78 percent of consumers, and over 92 percent of builders offer them in new homes (*Professional Builder 1985*).

Today, the dishwasher comes with electronic controls that allow the user to set it for various functions, a tremendous time saver.

Dishwashers that fit under the sink are now on the market (Figure 41). Some are a mere 18 inches wide, so the smallest kitchen can be equipped with one.

The standard dishwasher is 34½ inches high, 24 inches wide, and about 24 inches deep from front to back. It is designed to fit into a base cabinet. Panel fronts and glass doors are available.

Countertops

Today a host of countertop materials afford opportunities to turn mundane kitchens into showplaces. The favorite of 79 percent of consumers surveyed is plastic laminate, now made with color-through edging that eliminates the unsightly black line that marred the smooth look of countertops for years (*Kitchen and Bath Business* 1984).

Countertops need not be homogeneous. Use various materials to satisfy specific needs in the kitchen, such as a marble insert for a baking center, butcher block counter space for the food preparation center, or tile on an island cook top and eating center. Plan for the countertops when designing the kitchen so that cabinets can be properly designed for any special materials.

The possibilities are limited only by imagination and budget. An unimaginative countertop ruins the effect of the handsomest cabinets, but an attractive counter enhances any cabinet.

Countertops should be usually 3/4 to 1 inch wider than the standard 24-inch (front to back) counter, providing an overhang on the base cabinet. Standard cabinets are 36 inches high, including the countertop, proportioned for the average person. Appliances as well as base cabinets are standardized for this height.

If installing a cabinet taller than 36 inches, adjust for the unsightly overhang of the countertop where it meets the taller cabinet by mitering or curving the protruding edge back to the tall unit or by flushing out the shallow unit to meet the overhang.

Sections of counters may be placed at a 30-inch height for pastry and bread making or for seated work.

The backsplash or protective panel on the wall must meet the countertop. The standard backsplash is 4 inches deep but can extend to the cabinets. Backsplashes can be of material that is the same as or different from the countertop. If they are of the same material, the most desirable construction is the coved top, which curves up the backsplash and over the front edge. This eliminates seams and the necessity for caulking between the backsplash and the countertop. If a wall is made of tile, glass brick, or any material that cannot be harmed by water or grease, no backsplash is necessary.

Materials for countertops include laminates, ceramic, tile, stainless steel, marble, Corian, slate, granite, butcher block, or wood. Each has features to suit a multitude of needs and tastes.

Of the plastic laminates, the most generally known brands are Formica™, Wilsonart™, and Nevamar™, although many firms manufacture them. Laminates lend themselves to a variety of combinations. Contrasting effects can be achieved with edging and backsplashes. Inserts of other materials are easy to install in a counter, and laminates work well with tile and butcher block, as well as marble. Install laminates over plywood rather than sheetrock.

Laminates are easy to clean, heat resistant, and come in a wide range of prices, grades, and colors and styles, such as wood grains, marble effects, high-lacquer, and metalics. (See Figures 42 and 43.) On the other hand, laminates can be scratched and cannot be used as cutting surfaces.

One of the oldest decorative arts known to man, ceramic tile has added beauty and pleasure to homes for millenia. Whether hand made or mass produced, tile is increasingly popular for kitchen countertops, backsplashes, and decorative trim. In luxury kitchens, it was the choice of 24 percent of respondents to a

Courtesy General Electric

Figure 41. An undersink dishwasher is a space saver in a small kitchen.

Courtesy Wilsonart

Figure 42. Laminate countertop

Courtesy Wilsonart

Figure 43. This kitchen features natural-looking, synthetic countertops and wooden flooring.

Courtesy Betsy Godfrey

Figure 44. Tile countertop

survey conducted by *Kitchen and Bath Business* in 1984.

Install tile properly to prevent cracking. This means that the counter decking has to be plumb and sturdy. It must allow for expansion and contraction or else the tile and grout will crack. If plywood decking is used, it should be cut randomly. The surface must be flat and straight. Tile does not give, and any defects in the level of the surface will be evident.

Bullnose and edge pieces of tile are available, or you can use a wooden facer strip, installed prior to laying the tile. The facer must be finished and sealed before tiling because the grout will seep into the wood.

Tile is easy to clean, it does not burn, and it's available in an enormous variety of colors and patterns. It may be hand painted for custom-built homes. It does, however, crack and chip, and it's more expensive than laminates.

Stainless steel is generally thought of as institutional looking, but it's extremely practical. It is, however, usually used in commercial properties.

Stainless steel does not crack, chip, or burn, but it requires extra care to keep it looking stainless. Water spots are a particular problem.

It also causes fatigue if used for chopping because it has no give, and it dulls knives rapidly.

Marble is available in quarry marble or man-made versions. Quarry marble comes in all natural marble colors, including white, black, rose, brown, green, and grey. It is heavy and expensive and can be scratched and cracked and is difficult to maintain due to its porosity. Because it remains cool, it is highly desirable for pastry making. Inserts of marble in a mixing center make an excellent baking area. Marble requires plumb, sturdy counter decking because it is heavy and cannot be shimmed.

Marble produces handsome, elegant counters that do not burn. It does, however, require waxing and polishing to maintain its appearance.

Cultured marble, a synthetic resin with marble chips, doesn't get stained or etched from acids, but it can be scratched. It is generally not used for kitchens.

Synthetic marble, or Corian, looks like marble, although it is completely synthetic. It can be cut like wood with a power saw and router. Corian is waterproof, so it does not warp or rot. It resists heat and stains. If it is scratched or chipped, it can be repaired by buffing and sanding. Corian is so tough it has a ballistics rating. A solid cast sheet of a rigid acrylic, Corian is homogeneous, with no edges. It lends itself to highly decorative treatments. Corian seaming materials make any jointing virtually invisible.

Cabinets must be level to install Corian because it cannot be shimmed as laminates can. Installing under decking is necessary, just as it is for tile and marble. Corian comes in 1/4-, 1/2-, and 3/4-inch thicknesses. If the 1/2-inch thickness is used for the countertop, it is going to make the counter 35 inches high, rather than the usual 36 inches high. Installation must compensate for this with heavier counter decking or custom cabinets 35-1/2 inches high.

Slate makes a handsome countertop, particularly in rustic kitchens, but it is expensive. It can be bought in squares or slabs and is available in many natural colors from black to green. Installing slate requires an expert, just as tile installation does. In addition, slate gets cracked and nicked and cannot be repaired.

Granite is a heavy, attractive, and costly stone for a countertop that requires special cabinet support for its weight. It cannot be stained and is not damaged by moisture or heat. It shines when polished and comes in earth tones, pinks, reds, blues, and greens.

Butcher block makes a handsome counter and is excellent as an insert to add versatility and interest to countertops. It requires a strong cabinet base because

Courtesy Armstrong World Industries, Inc.

Figure 45. No-wax vinyl floor tiles.

it's heavy. It is actually a hardwood laminated under pressure. Install butcher block either as a drop-in or with a stainless steel ring. Take care to seal seams between materials because dirt gets caught in them and makes cleaning difficult. Hard rock sugar maple is the hardest and most impervious to cutting and scratching.

Wooden countertops are different from butcher block counters because they are sealed and finished with stain and varnish. They are good looking with wooden cabinets, as well as with laminates. They can be stained to match cabinets and are easy for the home owner to repair. They do, however, get scratched and scorched and can burn.

Floors

The floor in the kitchen is of utmost importance from both the aesthetic and the practical viewpoints. No one today wants a floor that requires waxing and special attention.

Floorings come in two classifications: the resilient type, which gives to the footstep and is comfortable to walk on, and the nonresilient type, which has no give but generally wears extremely well.

Selecting kitchen flooring depends on the price of the home. Generally, a vinyl floor is the best bet for the average home. Consumers of floors in all price ranges who chose their own floor coverings selected vinyl 59 percent of the time (*Kitchen and Bath Business* 1984).

Choice of the next favorite material depends on the market segment. Fourteen percent in the luxury market selected ceramic tile, and another 14 percent selected wooden floors. Nationally, however, 11 percent chose carpeting, with the lower market end selecting it 17 percent of the time (*Kitchen and Bath Business* 1984).

Geographical location affects the choice of material. For example, Pacific Coast customers like both tile and wood, while 72 percent of the West North Central customers opt for resilient flooring (*Kitchen and Bath Business 1984*).

Resilient Floor Materials

Comfort, practicality, and beauty probably account for the popularity of the favorite material, resilient vinyl, which wears extremely well. It requires only an occasional polishing and is easily cleaned. Vinyls come in a wide variety of colors and patterns to answer decorative needs.

Vinyl is available in both sheets and in tiles. Most builders prefer the sheet because it is usually less expensive. Sheet vinyl comes in various depths of cushioning, depending on the quality, to add resiliency and greater comfort. The no-wax vinyls are highly desirable and add sales appeal to the home.

For centuries, wooden floors served throughout the home, including the kitchen, and today, many people still prefer these for beauty, longevity, and resiliency. A top-quality polyurethane finish makes wood impervious to water, grease, and other spills. Consider a wooden floor for a luxury kitchen.

Relatively inexpensive, carpeting gives an instant look of luxury and provides a soft, resilient surface. Indoor carpeting, however, is hard to keep as clean as vinyl or wood, is not as long-wearing, and is susceptible to stains. It's probably not a good installation for anything but a custom-built home where the client requests it.

Nonresilient Floor Materials

Although considered a luxury, ceramic tile can be competitive with top-quality vinyl or wooden floors. Handsome and decorative, ceramic tiles are harder on the feet and can be noisy. If a breakable item is dropped on such a floor, the item will certainly break, whereas on a resilient floor, it might not. Dropped heavy items will break the tile as well.

Tile requires a strong, firm base and can be laid over a concrete subfloor or plywood if proper precautions are taken. The floor surface must be flat to prevent cracking of tile and/or grout. Be sure to coordinate the grout color with the tile and seal the grout.

Vinyl-bonded tiles are more resilient and therefore easier on the feet and quieter. Quarry tile can also be used but must be sealed to prevent staining. Save this for custom-built kitchens, usually with a country or Spanish flavor.

Slate or brick are hard materials, durable and attractive. Subfloors must be strong enough to carry this weight. Both of these need flat surfaces underneath them to prevent cracking. These are for luxury or custom-built kitchens.

Courtesy Wood-Mode Cabinetry

Figure 46. Wooden flooring. (Note also the pull-out table.)

Courtesy Summitville Tile

Figure 47. Tile flooring

Chapter 6
Lighting

Anyone who remembers an old-fashioned kitchen with its one ceiling light understands the need for good lighting. Unfortunately, even in many modern kitchens the lighting is poorly planned, contributing to accidents and fatigue.

A marketable kitchen is planned with two types of lighting: general and work lighting. General lighting bathes a room with light and eliminates deep shadows. It can also provide special accents with dimmer switches or be supplemented with chandeliers or spots. Work lighting should be provided for specific kitchen tasks, such as cooking, cleaning up, and mixing.

General Lighting

The amount of light needed depends on the size of the room. Guidelines for general lighting established by General Electric Company appear in Table 4.

Table 4-Recommended Lighting Requirements

Room Size	*Surface-mounted Fixtures*	*Recessed Units (12"-bottom minimum)*
less than 75 sq. ft.	60-65W fluorescent	80W
	150W incandescent	two 150W
75 - 120 sq. ft.	60-80W fluorescent	80W
	150-200W incandescent	400W
more than 120 sq. ft.	.25W/sq. ft. fluorescent	80-120W/sq. ft.
	2W/sq. ft. incandescent	150W/40 sq. ft.

Fluorescent light provides the best, most economical light because it gives more illumination per watt at the lowest price. Fluorescent lights have an average life ranging from 9,000 hours to 20,000 hours; incandescent bulbs last from 750 to 2,500 hours (for the extended-life variety). Furthermore, over 56 percent of home buyers prefer fluorescent lights (*Professional Builder* 1985).

Completely shield light fixtures and place them in the center of the kitchen, close to the ceiling with diffusing glass or plastic shades. The new, warm fluorescent lights are preferable because they flatter the tones in wooden cabinets, the room in general, and the color of food and complexions.

Perimeter lighting may also be used as general lighting. If using tracks or other perimeter lights, place them 18 to 24 inches out from the cabinet edge. The minimum amount of fluorescent lighting needed in a square kitchen is two 48-inch, 40-watt lights; an L-shaped kitchen requires four 36-inch, 30-watt lights. The minimum wattage required for incandescent track lights is 40- to 60-watt, white, 5-inch-diameter G-bulbs, 24 to 30 inches apart. The ceiling should be painted flat white; do not use directional units.

Accent lights may enhance general lighting practically and aesthetically. For example, a chandelier placed over a counter provides a visual separation between the work area and the rest of the house. One placed over a table defines the area and adds to the appeal of the room. Use a dimmer switch on such chandeliers to regulate the light for different uses.

Decorative chandeliers, such as wrought iron ones with pot hooks or Tiffany-like lamps, are primarily used as accents over tables, counters, or islands with downdraft cook tops. If used as the central fixture, be sure to provide enough additional light to make the room functional.

Hang chandeliers 30 inches above the table surface in a room with an 8-foot ceiling. For each additional foot of ceiling height, raise the chandelier 3 inches. A 9-foot ceiling, for example, requires a chandelier 33 inches above the table. A downlight chandelier should not extend to the edge of the counter or table. Place it 24 inches back from the edge to prevent glare and discomfort from heat. The circumference of the fixture should be 12 inches less than the width of the table.

Remember that light walls and counters reflect light, and dark ones absorb it. If dark woods and paint are used, increase the amount of light.

Work Lighting

No matter how handsome a kitchen, it is a working room, and proper lighting is crucial for safety, comfort, and convenience.

Ceiling fixtures bathe the entire room and are essential for good lighting, but the minute a body comes between the light and the working surface, it casts a shadow. (See Figure 49.) Therefore, the best light for working is under-cabinet light.

The range hood may provide light for the stove and should accommodate the equivalent of at least two 75-watt bulbs. If there is no hood, two 75-watt incandescent reflectors or two 36-inch, 30-watt fluorescent lights should provide enough light. (The recommended placement of a range hood at 60 inches from the floor prevents the light from glaring into the eyes

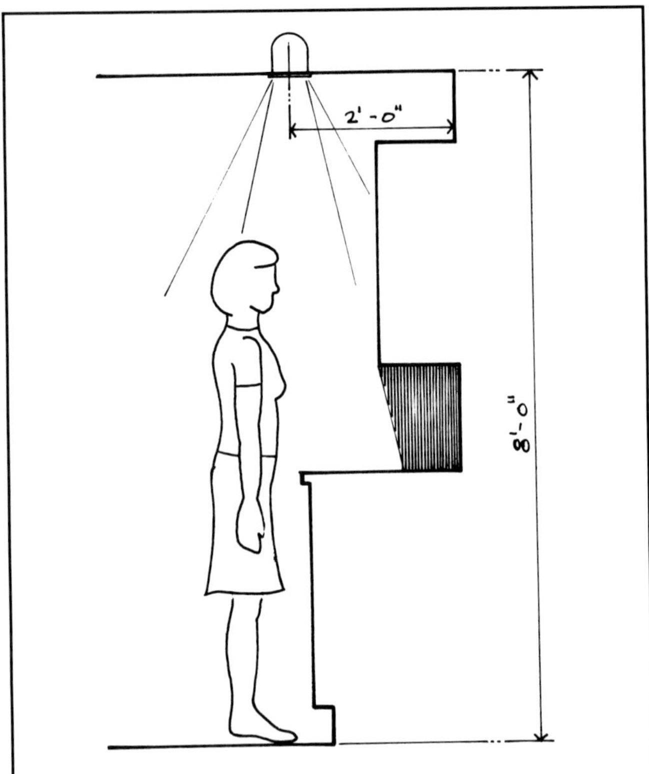

Figure 49A. The light from this ceiling fixture is blocked by the cabinet.

of the average-height woman.)

Fluorescent lights installed over the sink may be either recessed or surface mounted, with a shielded fixture, or exposed tubes placed behind a faceboard 8 inches deep. Two 36-inch, 30-watt or three 24-inch, 20-watt lights should suffice. If using recessed or surface-mounted incandescent downlights, space them 15 inches apart, with a minimum of two 75-watt reflector floods or two 100-watt bulbs with reflectors in the fixture. Center the lights over the sink.

Counter work areas are best lighted by fluorescent under-cabinet lights installed as close to the front of the cabinet as possible. Use the longest tube that will fit. The fixture bracket should cover at least two-thirds of the length of the cabinet.

Track lights and spots won't replace under-cabinet lights in specific areas. Good-looking and practical for contemporary designs, track lights are set on open or closed channels. The open channel is more flexible because lights can be changed easily and direction can be shifted. The closed channel tracks work well when no flexibility is needed; they are also easier to clean because no grease collects in the track.

In addition to artificial light, a skylight in the kitchen adds great sales appeal, as do bay and greenhouse windows. Or build a window wall facing a garden between the counter and the cabinets for an outstanding effect. Glass brick creates a light-filled wall and can be inserted on a wall where a window is impractical.

Courtesy Whirlpool

Figure 48. Proper chandelier placement ensures efficient lighting. The skylight and glass brick enhance the lighting in this kitchen as well.

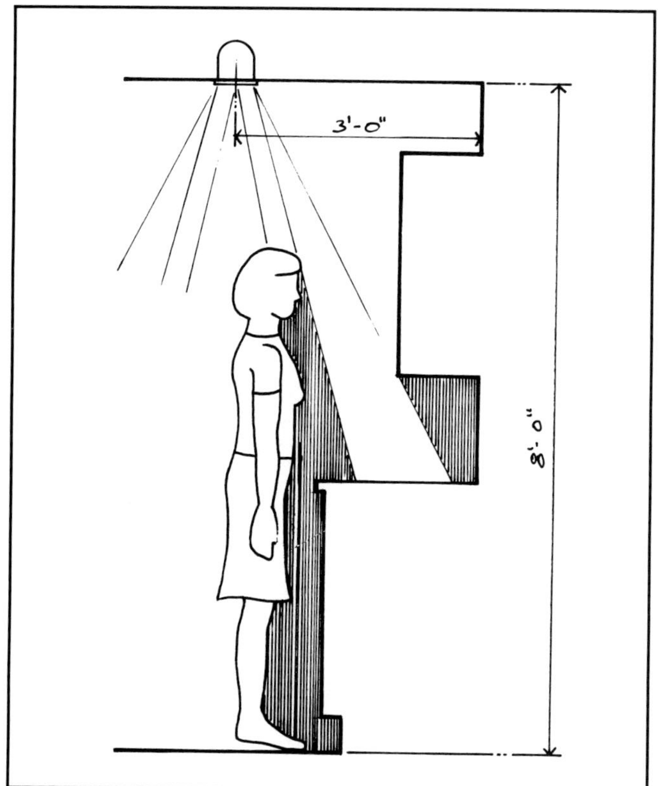

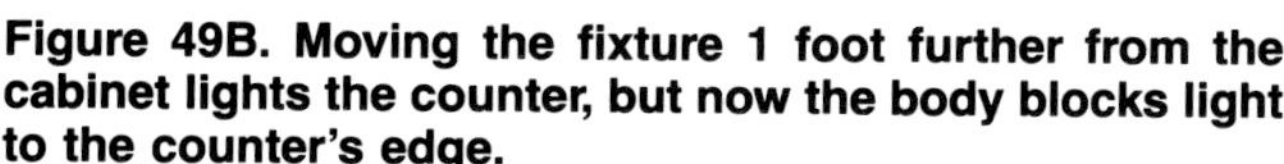

Figure 49B. Moving the fixture 1 foot further from the cabinet lights the counter, but now the body blocks light to the counter's edge.

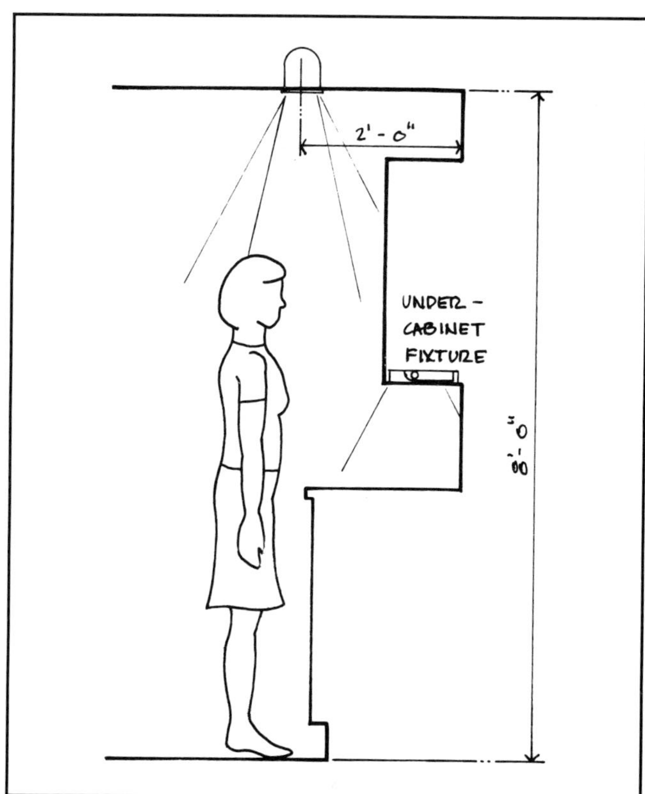

Figure 49C. Under-cabinet light floods the entire counter-top.

Chapter 7

Ventilation

The heat and steam in a kitchen can be exhausting as well as unpleasant. Not only does a well-ventilated kitchen prevent fatigue, it saves energy and thus, money.

In addition, good ventilation reduces moisture, smoke, and cooking odors that drift through the house. Grease particles can be carried by moisture droplets and smoke, damaging fabrics and wooden finishes, as well as making maintenance difficult.

Today's tightly sealed houses are more susceptible to damage from excess moisture than ever before. In older houses, moisture leaks out. In new ones, it stays in, damaging interiors and furnishings.

Kitchens can be ventilated with wall or ceiling fans or with hood and fan combinations. Of these alternatives, the hood and fan is the most efficient way to remove the moisture, smoke, and odors from the kitchen. Hoods trap the contaminants, and the fan exhausts them from the room. Hoods are attractively designed to add decoration and practicality. Custom and stock hoods are available.

The efficiency of a fan is based on the number of times per hour that it changes the air in a room, measured in cubic feet per minute (CFM). An effective fan should change the air once every four minutes or 15 times an hour, the accepted standard. The Home Ventilating Institute (HVI) has developed ratings for the CFM of a unit, found on unit labels.

In addition to rating hoods, HVI also measures hood noise in sones. The sone is an internationally recognized measurement of loudness. One sone is equivalent to the sound of a quiet refrigerator in a quiet kitchen. At a sone level of 4, conversation is difficult. A 2 range is preferable. Multispeed fans alleviate noise pollution, because they can be turned up or down, depending on the amount of power needed.

Hood Fans

Hoods should extend at least the length of the cook top, and decorative hoods look best if they extend 6 inches beyond the cook top. Hoods should be a minimum of 17 inches from front to back and as close to the cook top as possible without obstructing vision. The user must have a clear view of the back burners and not be in danger of hitting the hood with his/her head. The standard recommended distance from the floor to the bottom of the hood is 56 to 60 inches. (See Figure 51.)

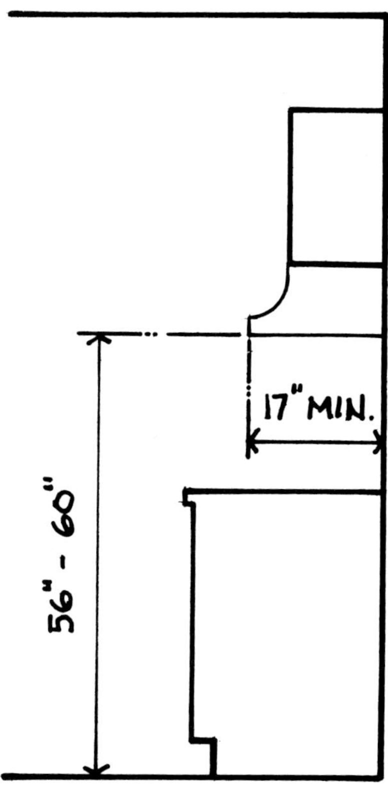

Figure 50. Recommended dimensions for range hoods

Courtesy Broan Manufacturing Company

Figure 51. This hood serves both a practical and a decorative function.

A hood set across a 45-degree corner should be at least 36 inches wide or 6 inches wider than the cook top, and it should be set 6 inches back from the junction of the base cabinet.

The CFM of hood fans is determined by the size of the hood. Hood fans should have the following capacities:

- A wall-installed range hood should have 100 CFMs per linear foot of hood. Thus, a 36-inch hood requires 360 CFMs. The formula for this is 3 feet X 100 CFM = 300 CFM.
- An island or peninsula range hood should have 120 CFMs per linear foot. Thus, a 36-inch cook top requires 360 CFMs. The formula is 3 feet X 120 CFM= 360 CFM.

The maximum HVI rating for sones is 8 for a kitchen hood with up to 500-CFM capacity.
to the outside. Non-ducted hoods can remove odors but do not remove heat and moisture. As a matter of fact, tests done for the FHA at Kansas State University show that non-ducted hoods can cause more grease to accumulate on kitchen walls than no hood at all (National Kitchen and Bath Association 1984). Built-in ovens should also have exhaust fans, particularly for broiling when the door is open.

Wall and Ceiling Fans

If, for any reason, a hood cannot be installed, and a wall or ceiling fan must be substituted, the CFM required can be calculated by multiplying the square footage of the kitchen floor by two, based on an 8-foot ceiling height. Thus, a 130-square-foot kitchen needs an exhaust fan with a 260-CFM rating based on this formula: 130 X 2 = 260 CFM.

A ceiling fan helps circulation and is a good decorative touch but will not serve the same function as an exhaust fan.

Plan kitchens so that natural breezes can help ventilate them in seasonable weather. But remember to keep drafts away from stoves.

Chapter 8

The Basic Kitchen

Even a small kitchen includes the basic appliances and other amenities. It's a case of the smaller the home, the smaller the kitchen. Every inch of floor space must be used to its best advantage. Plan carefully to ensure that doors open properly, adequate counter space and storage space are provided, and, most importantly, that the kitchen is appealing to the eye as well as functional.

Units of less than 1,000 square feet are considered basic in size, according to the Small Homes Council - Building Research Council. Generally, the target market for homes of this size is the first-time buyer. Empty-nesters (55 and older) are also potential buyers but often expect more luxury.

The first-time home buyer and the empty-nesters want many of the same things as the move-up buyer, but may prefer a different emphasis. Some amenities that both groups want are the following:

- Visually open kitchen with a divider (next to the family room is the second choice)
- Special use storage
- Walk-in pantry
- Mop, broom, and shelf space
- Bay window
- More counter space
- Island counter space
- Countertop microwave

Providing these features on a limited budget in a tight space can be a problem. The preference for open design works in your favor, because it offers ways to achieve a sense of space. Changing a solid wall into a peninsula or other counter arrangement offers one quick solution. This satisfies the buyer's desire for an open design and creates a more spacious look at the same time.

To start with, the kitchen must include the three basic appliances—sink, range, and refrigerator. Dishwashers also can be included under the sink in the smallest kitchen, or they can be placed beside the sink. This fourth appliance should be standard, except in homes in the lowest end of the market.

Courtesy Betsy Godfrey

Figure 52. This basic kitchen has been enhanced with a pass-through.

A microwave can be added with little additional cost. Putting it in a wall cabinet or a combination range saves counter space and adds a selling advantage to the house. Microwave cabinetry is available from most manufacturers. Wiring for microwaves must be planned for in designing floor plans.

The following examples show how rearrangement of appliances and design improvements in the four types of kitchen layouts open up the space, making it much more imaginative.

U-shape

The U-shape kitchen is the most desirable. In Figure

53, the kitchen is 108 inches X 102 inches (9 feet X 8 feet, 6 inches). The work triangle is 13 feet, 6 inches, and a 30-inch table area has been left beside the range. There are 72 inches of base cabinet frontage and 96 inches of countertop surface. Space above the mixing center is adequate for a microwave installation.

The kitchen works, but it's dull. It has all the necessary elements, including a dishwasher, but has a minimum of cabinet space.

If you turn the cabinet arm with the range into a peninsula and extend it, an additional 24 inches of base cabinet frontage is gained underneath the peninsula counter. The counter adds 30 inches of frontage, and more importantly, the room is now opened up to the adjacent living quarters. (See Figure 54.)

Since 30 inches accommodates only one seated person, the peninsula is rounded so that it is useful from both sides and the end. Three can now use it for eating, and it provides a convenient serving center beside the range.

If you hang cabinets above the peninsula, an additional 30 inches of wall cabinet frontage is gained.

L-shape

The kitchen in Figure 55, 96 inches X 132 inches, forms an 18-foot triangle among the work centers. A table in the corner creates a closed-in feeling. The minimum 26 inches of space (36 inches is better) necessary to push a chair back on one side is missing.

If you remove the side wall and substitute a 36-inch-high island with an 18-inch counter, you provide an eating and work counter that seats two, with 24 inches across for each, 15 to 18 inches of knee room, and the recommended 36 inches behind the chairs or stools. (See Figure 56.)

The island can be used while putting groceries into the refrigerator or taking them out, providing additional mixing center space. In the original design, the base cabinet frontage was 72 inches, and countertop frontage was 96 inches. The island adds 48 more inches of base cabinet frontage and increases the countertop frontage by 52 inches. In addition, the living quarters

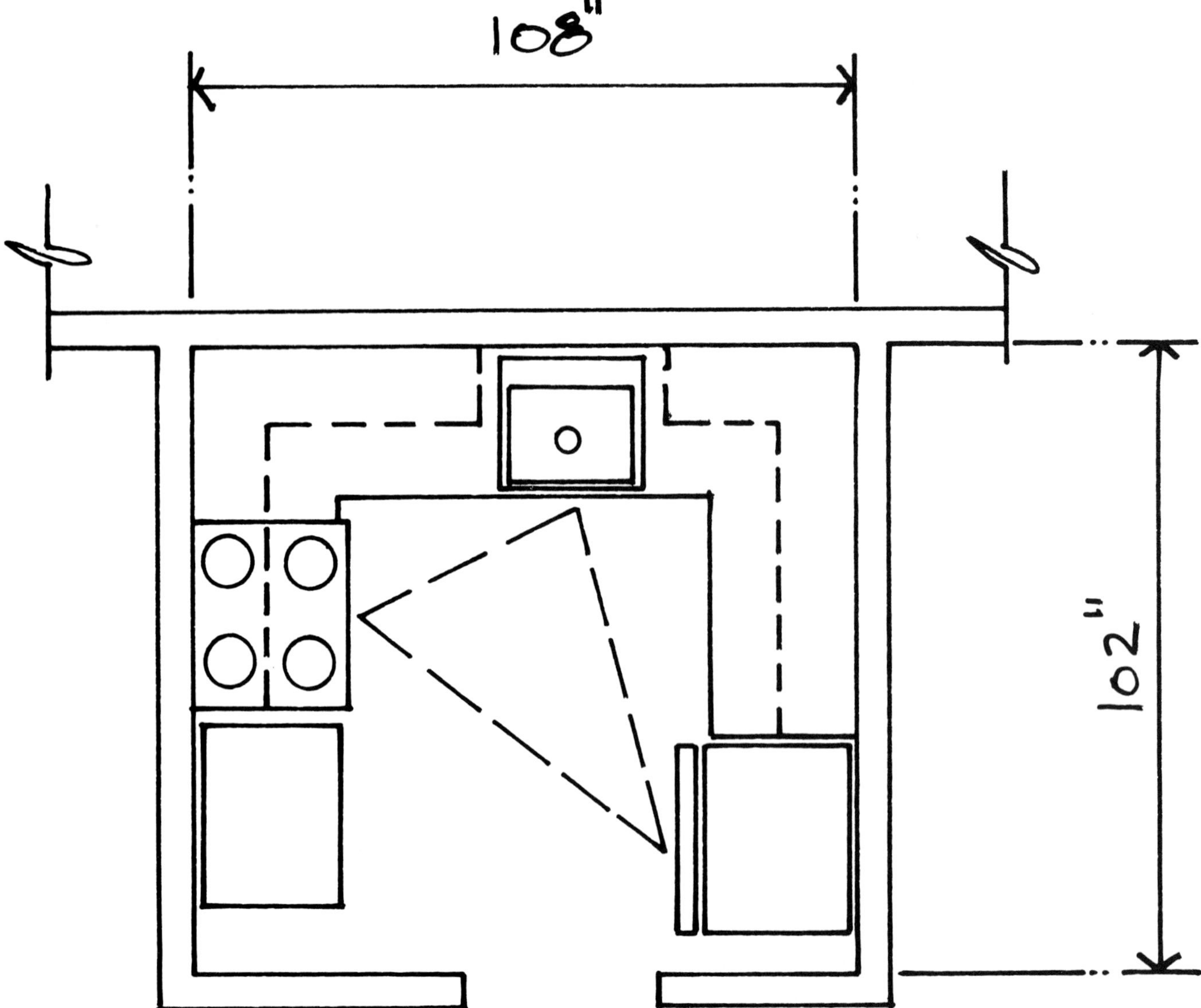

Figure 53. Basic U-shaped kitchen with work triangle – 13′ 6″, base cabinet frontage – 72″, counter top surface – 96″

look more spacious: the home has been opened up.

Turning the window above the sink into a small greenhouse window contributes to the open feeling and admits more light.

Two-Wall

In small spaces, the corridor arrangement is sometimes the only option. The corridor width must be at least 96 inches (8 feet) wide, which allows the 24 inches of depth required for cabinets on each side, plus 48 inches of clearance between the cabinet runs. The refrigerator extends further into the corridor area but is functional.

In Figure 58 the entire room is enclosed. Opening up the sink wall to the ceiling and adding a decorative device, such as cabinets suspended over the entire counter, make for interesting possibilities. A balanced arrangement of 24- X 30-inch cabinets above each end, with open shelves in the middle or shallow cabinets, also works well. Hanging cabinets should be usable from both sides. This design opens up the room, provides a seating area for three, and increases under-counter storage space.

One-Wall

The one-wall kitchen in Figure 60 is 186 inches X 72 inches (15 feet, 6 inches X 6 feet) and stretches the work triangle to 22 feet. The base cabinet frontage is the minimum 72 inches; wall cabinets are also 72 inches. Countertop frontage is 96 inches.

You can turn this design into an L-shaped room by cutting its length just 6 inches and increasing its width

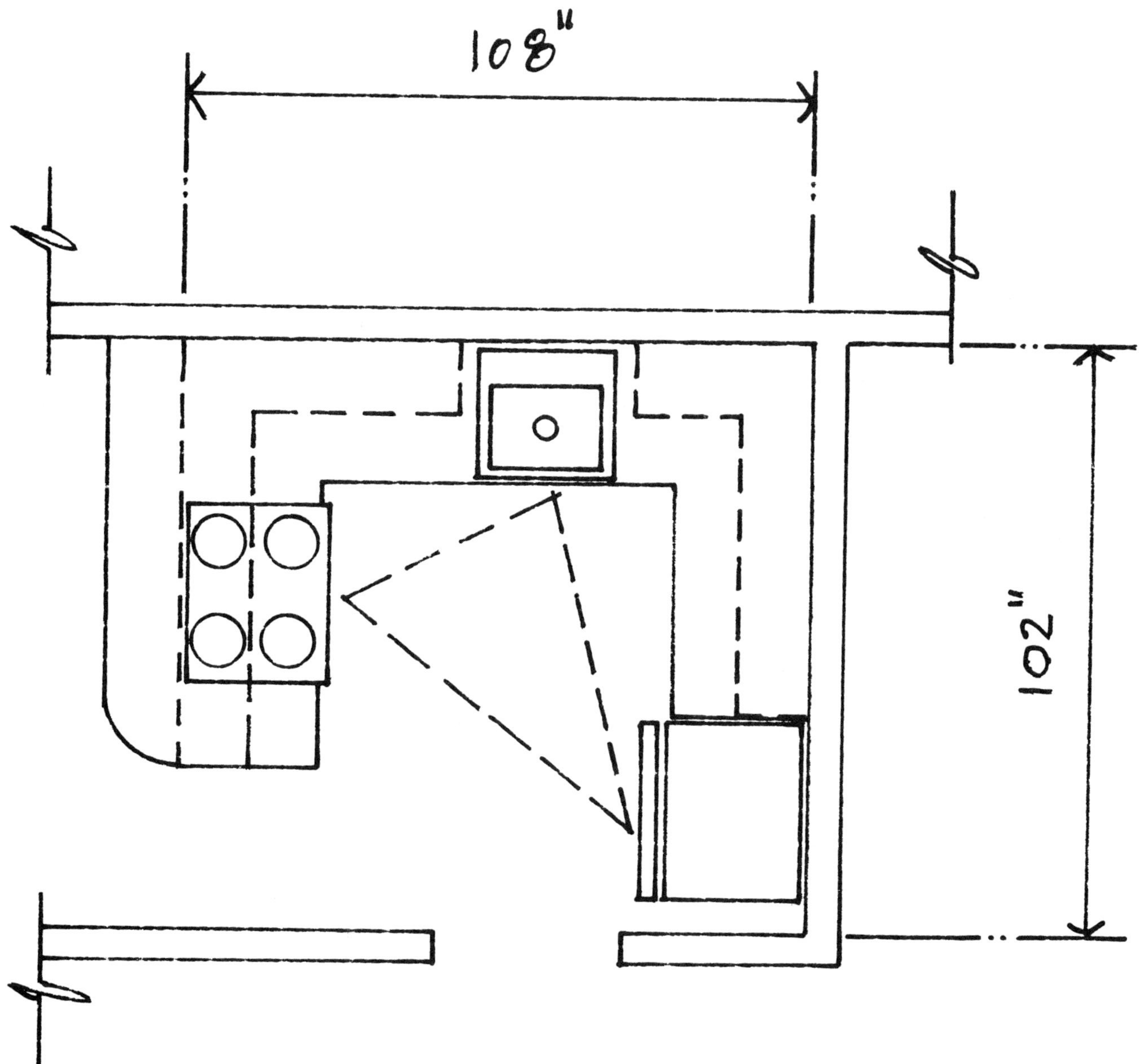

Figure 54. Basic U-shaped kitchen (revised) with work triangle – 13′5″, base cabinet frontage – 96″, countertop and eating surface – 162″

to 80 inches (7 feet, 6 inches). (See Figure 61.) This provides sufficient room to set up a narrow counter/ divider to separate the kitchen from the rest of the house. (This arrangement, however, increases the work triangle to 23 feet, 6 inches.)

Another alternative that makes space large enough for the counter or room divider and turns this into an eating area, is to reduce the room to 168 inches (14 feet) and widen it to 102 inches (8 feet, 6 inches), reducing the work triangle to 22 feet. Since the eating area is 90 inches (14 feet) in length, three people can be comfortably accommodated, and four can be squeezed in.

Both designs increase the base and wall cabinet frontage to 96 inches. Each of these arrangements has a good work triangle, uninterrupted by traffic flow.

Each kitchen has proper access to the outside and to the remainder of the house. The doors do not interfere with the appliances. The range is placed to give serving access to the eating area. The refrigerator is near the exterior door.

These designs provide a basic number of appliances. Yet it is simple to include a disposal in addition to a dishwasher and a microwave, giving a total of six appliances, rather than the basic three. By offering these, you have the opportunity to sell options and increase profits.

Furthermore, when the consumer sees that space has been allowed for an appliance, such as a microwave, homes are easier to sell. In addition, a base cabinet with a pull-out or fold-down table in a tight kitchen has invaluable sales appeal. Extras that add sales appeal are the following:

- Range with built-in microwave
- Disposal
- Dishwasher
- Pull-out or folding table
- Storage wall - shallow shelves built across blank wall
- Soffit over sink with built-in lights
- Lazy susan (drum carousel) in corner cabinet
- Roll-out under-sink storage
- Pull-out cutting board
- Built-in trash receptacle
- Trash compactor

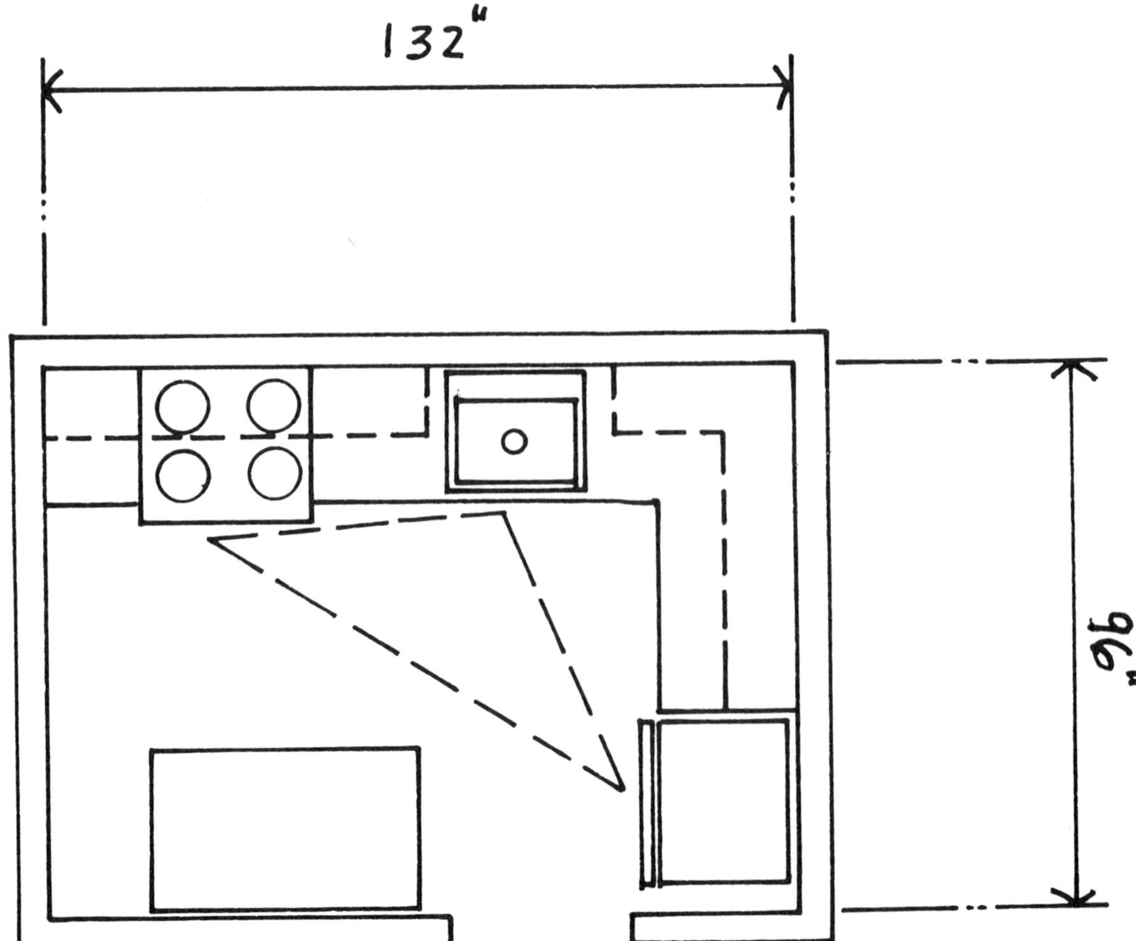

Figure 55. Basic L-shaped kitchen work triangle – 18″, base cabinet frontage – 72″, countertop surface – 96″

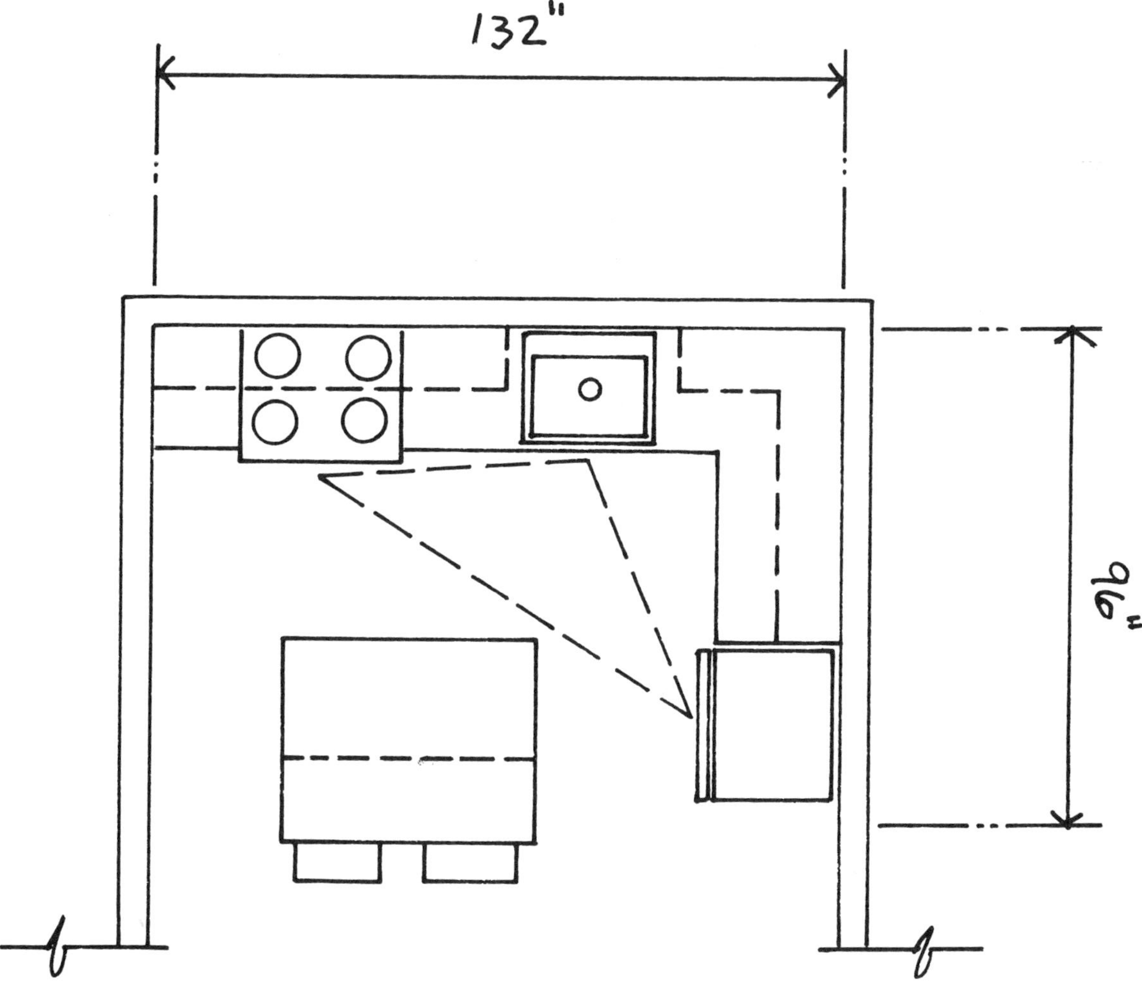

Figure 56. Basic L-shaped kitchen (revised) with work triangle – 18′, base cabinet frontage – 120″, countertop surface – 148″

Courtesy Wood-Mode Cabinetry

Figure 57. An Imaginative design enhances this basic kitchen.

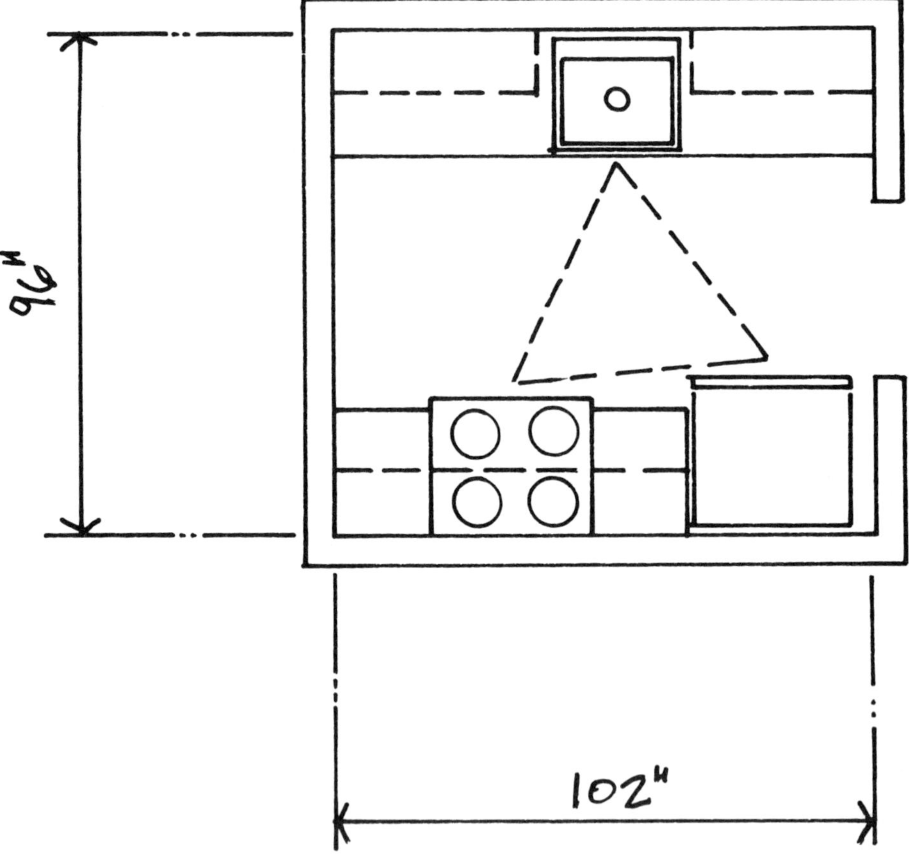

Figure 58. Basic two-wall kitchen with work triangle – 144″, base cabinet frontage – 108″, countertop surface – 108″

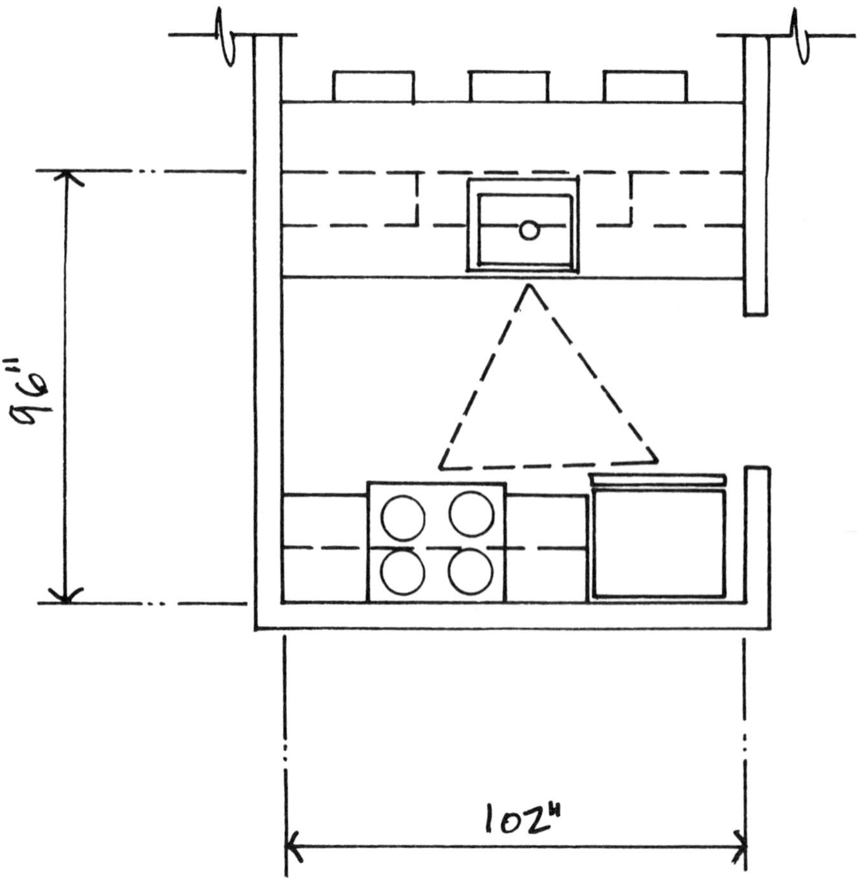

Figure 59. Basic two-wall kitchen (revised) with work triangle – 144″, base cabinet frontage – 114″, countertop surface – 204″

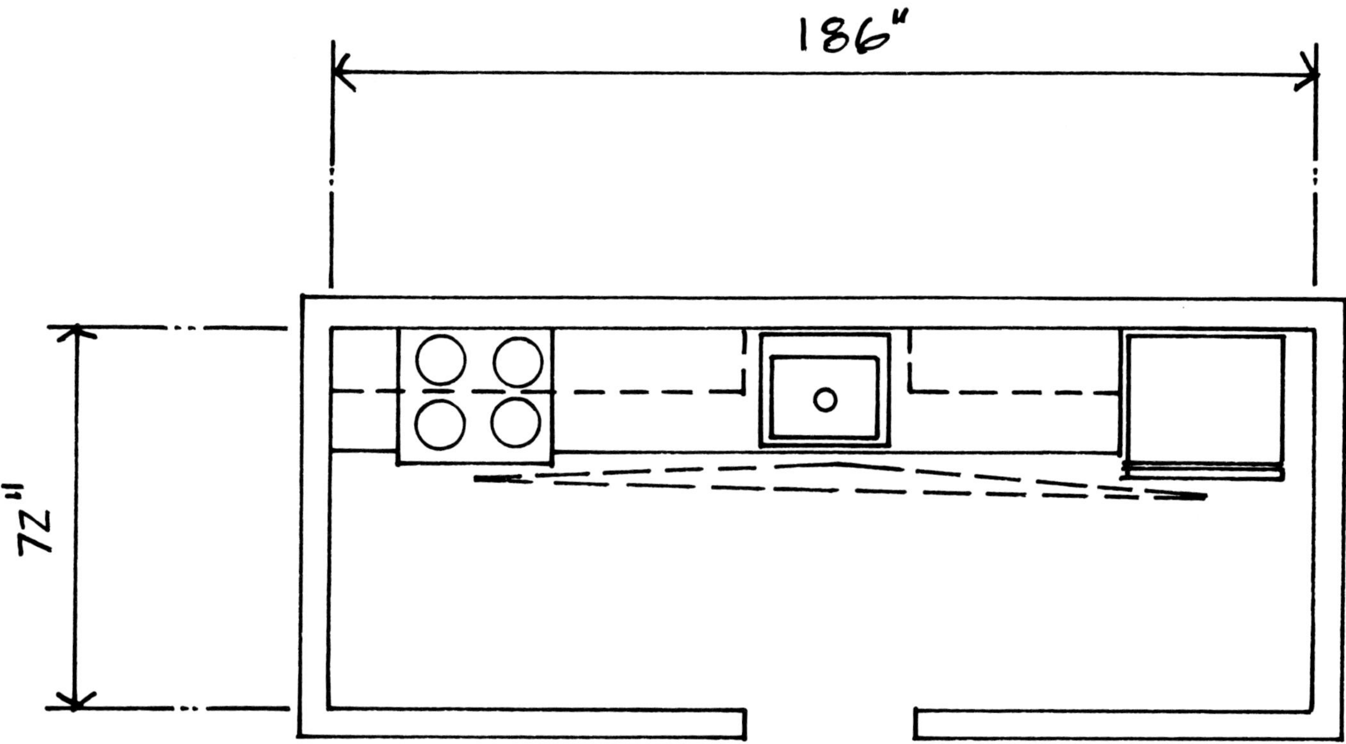

Figure 60. Basic one-wall kitchen with work triangle – 22′, base cabinet frontage – 72″, countertop surface – 96″

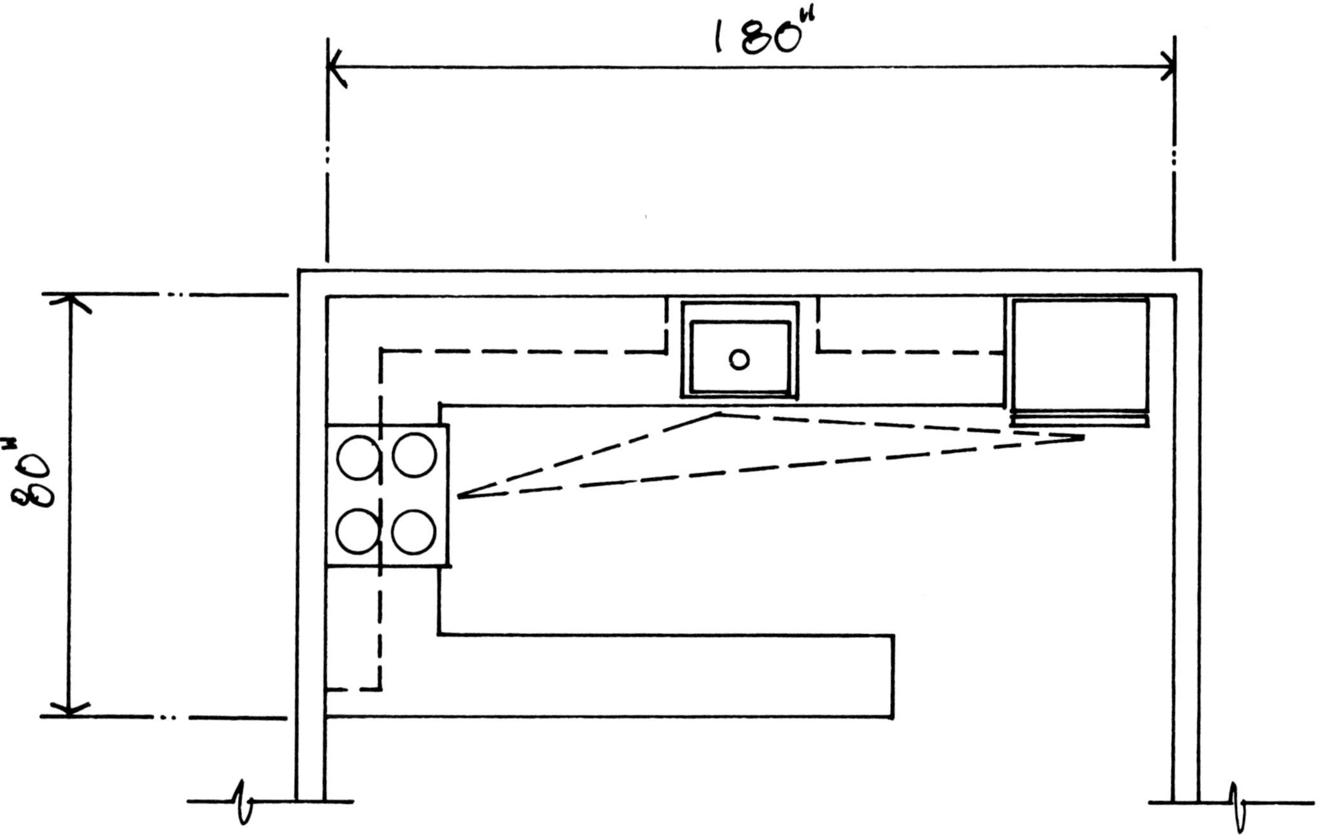

Figure 61. Basic one-wall kitchen (revised) with work triangle – 22′7″, base cabinet frontage – 90″, countertop surface – 186″

Chapter 9
The Move-Up Kitchen

Builders targeting the move-up market face enormous competition, as designers turn their talents toward ways to excite and lure buyers. Since builders have more to spend on move-up kitchens, successful designs are practical and appealing, with the amenities this market seeks.

Getting the most for the dollar starts with proper planning. Too often, the additional space in single-family homes is simply wasted. Square footage is increased, but the appliances are placed around the room without regard for work triangle size or the proper placement of the work centers.

Such a kitchen is just as inefficient as the huge, old-fashioned kitchen was, with a lot of wasted space in the center that forces the user to walk more. And too often, these kitchens are thoroughfares providing the only direct access from the utility section to the living section of the home.

The easiest way to visualize the difference between a well-planned kitchen and a poorly planned one is to analyze some examples. The following drawings give examples of each kitchen configuration, showing good and poor design.

U-shape

This preferred shape is easily adapted and created by imaginative use of space. Consider a traditional square-shaped room with two doors (Figure 63). The sample room is 12 feet X 11 feet, 6 inches, with an 18-foot work triangle.

Note the placement of the counters and appliances, which can be rearranged to increase efficiency and usefulness. To create a more open design, preferred by consumers, add a visual divider.

For better design, remove part of the wall between the kitchen and the family room, adding a cook top on the remaining arm. (See Figure 64.) This increases the depth of the counter to give the required 15- to 18-inch overhang on the family room side, allowing space for both seating and for the cook top.

Courtesy St. Charles

Figure 62. Move-up kitchen

Move the refrigerator nearer to the sink, so that the work triangle is now 12 feet. Install in its place a pantry, and put the wall ovens on the same side, with ample space for a serving area beside the cook top counter. Round the corner to give a sense of more space. Install double-sided cabinets over the eating counter to store glasses and equipment for entertaining on the family room side. Set an accessory sink into the counter facing the family room; add a wine rack above.

L-shape

The sample L-shape kitchen, 16 feet X 16 feet, has a work triangle of 36 feet (Figure 65).

The center of the room is wasted space, demanding more walking on the part of the user. The refrigerator is next to the end wall, lacking counter space. (A double-door refrigerator is often used in a move-up kitchen.)

The range is on the far wall opposite the door, without counter space on the left side. The microwave is on the same wall, with a door that opens to the right; since counter space is lacking on the left, the door has to be closed before food can be put down.

The traffic pattern for this room is poor; the outside door is at the outside end of the room from the refrigerator.

To improve this kitchen, relocate the work centers (Figure 67). Move the cook top to an island; move the refrigerator further into the kitchen, allowing for a pantry and cabinet space on the right side and the mixing center on the left.

This reduces the work triangle to 19 feet, with 60 inches between the counter and the island. This allows ample room to open the appliance doors, for two people to pass each other, and for one person to work at the cook top while another is at the mixing center, even though this is not really a two-cook kitchen.

Add counter space for four at the island, dropping a hood over the area to make a visual divider between the work space and the living space. (This provides the divider that 46 percent of the market prefers.)

The kitchen now has room for a table and chairs in a small dining area. Extend the counter for additional storage space, open shelves, and optional cabinets. In a custom home, for example, the buyer might desire a sewing cabinet in this space. Or it is ideal for a cabinet that contains a serving cart.

The table is 48 inches in diameter, with 36 inches between the table edge and the wall so that the chairs can be pushed back.

The counter is 36 inches high at the eating area, which permits the use of stools 24 to 25 inches high. It extends 12 inches from the base, providing sufficient knee room. The area behind it is 24 inches, leaving room to move the stools.

Other alternatives with this space include turning the counter into an angled peninsula that extends to form an eating area for four people. The cook top is then removed from this part of the counter and placed back further. A downdraft cook top eliminates the need for a hood, but work lights would have to be installed.

The eating area has a chandelier. This part of the counter has been lowered to table height. For use with stools, the counter height remains the same. Lowering it, however, provides the sense of a separate dining

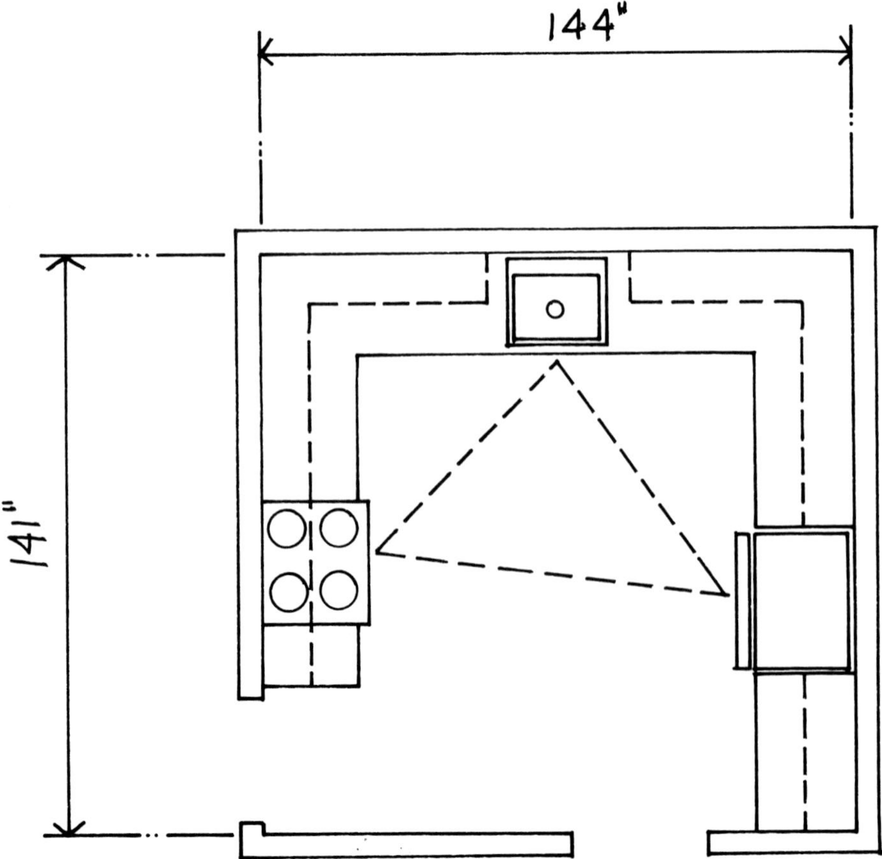

Figure 63. Move-up U-shaped kitchen with work triangle – 18′, base cabinet frontage – 168″, countertop surface – 208″

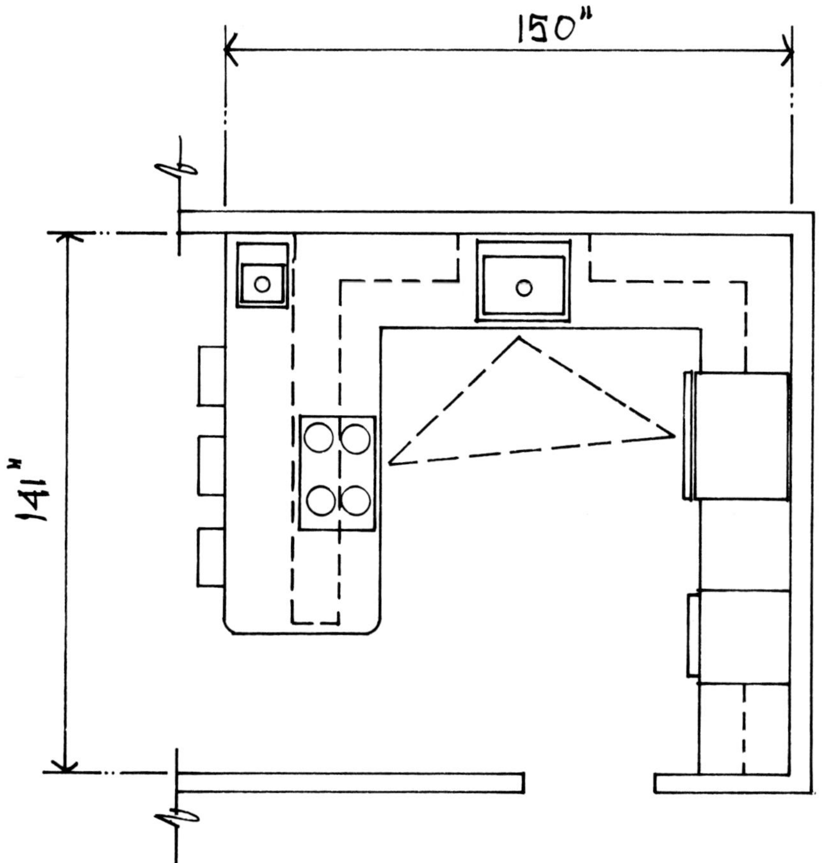

Figure 64. Move-up U-shaped kitchen (revised) with work triangle – 12′, base cabinet frontage – 144″, countertop surface – 305″

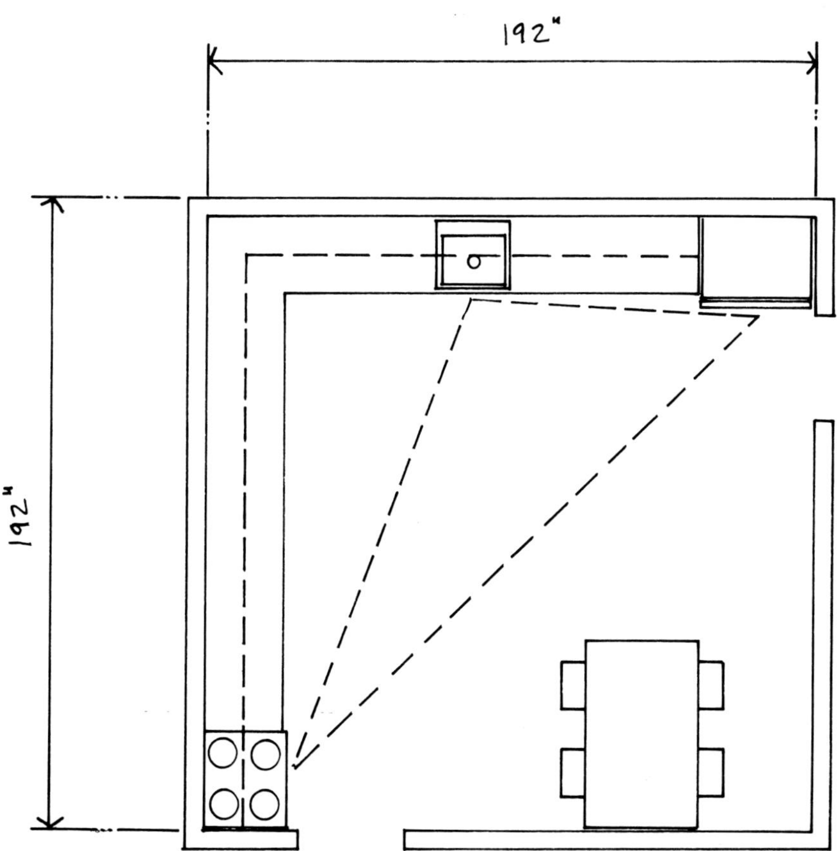

Figure 65. Move-up L-shaped kitchen with work triangle – 36′, base cabinet frontage – 216″, countertop surface – 240″

area, enhanced by the chandelier.

This L-shape kitchen has essentially become a U-shape. Traffic flows along the wall corridor without obstructing the path to the stove, sink, or mixing areas.

Two Wall

Some corridor, or two-wall, kitchens present problems due to their small sizes. These are usually found in homes, such as condominiums, with minimal square footage that are not necessarily lower-priced homes. Furthermore, sometimes kitchens in large homes are so badly designed that the work triangle is large and inefficient.

Traffic patterns also present a particular problem in the corridor kitchen. Proper planning of the whole house prevents the corridor kitchen, however, from becoming a thoroughfare. If floor plans place the kitchen in this predicament, the only solution is to change the plan, relocating the room or providing for an alternate traffic flow.

A typical corridor arrangement, 14 feet X 30 feet, has alternatives for more convenience and better aesthetics (Figure 68).

In this sample the traffic pattern runs straight through the kitchen, disrupting the work triangle. The garage and utility room access are at the far end of the room, away from the refrigerator. The dining room door is at the other end, away from the cook top. The breakfast table is in what should be the working end of the room, near the dining room.

Good planning improves this kitchen without redesigning the house. Relocate the cook top to a peninsula arm near the sink. Move the refrigerator to the garage door side of the room.

Place the ovens on the interior wall, out of the triangle, with plenty of counter space on either side. Cabinets by the oven are for dinnerware, serving pieces, and service for formal and informal dining. Place the microwave over the mixing center between

Courtesy Wood-Mode Cabinetry

Figure 66. Move-up kitchen

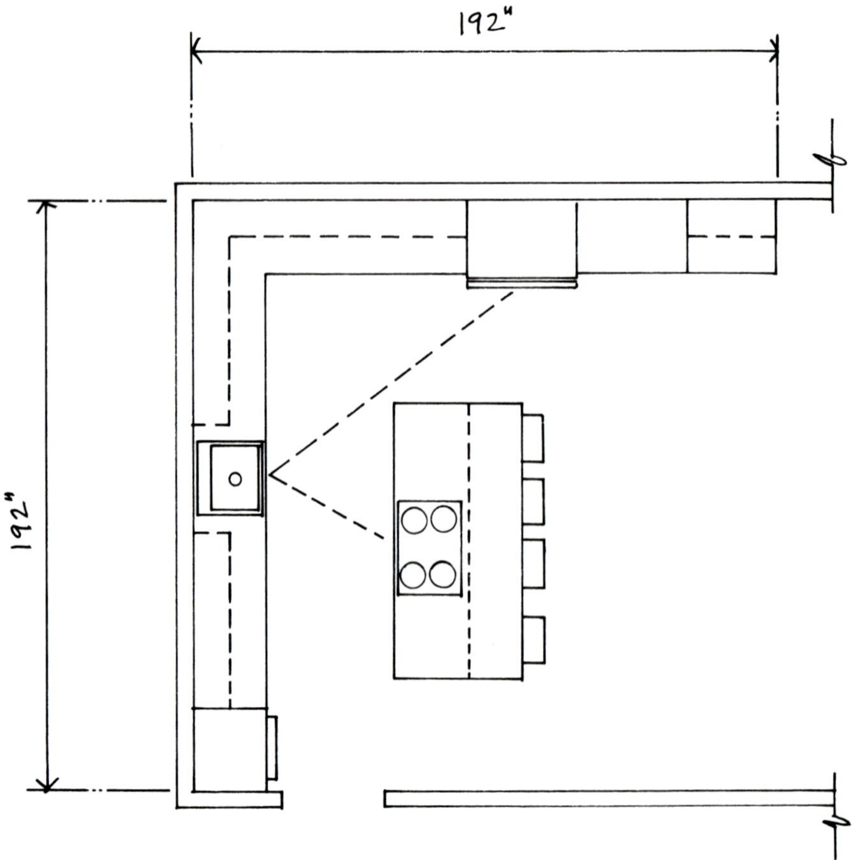

Figure 67. Move-up L-shaped kitchen (revised) with work triangle – 19′, base cabinet frontage – 264 ″, countertop surface – 354″

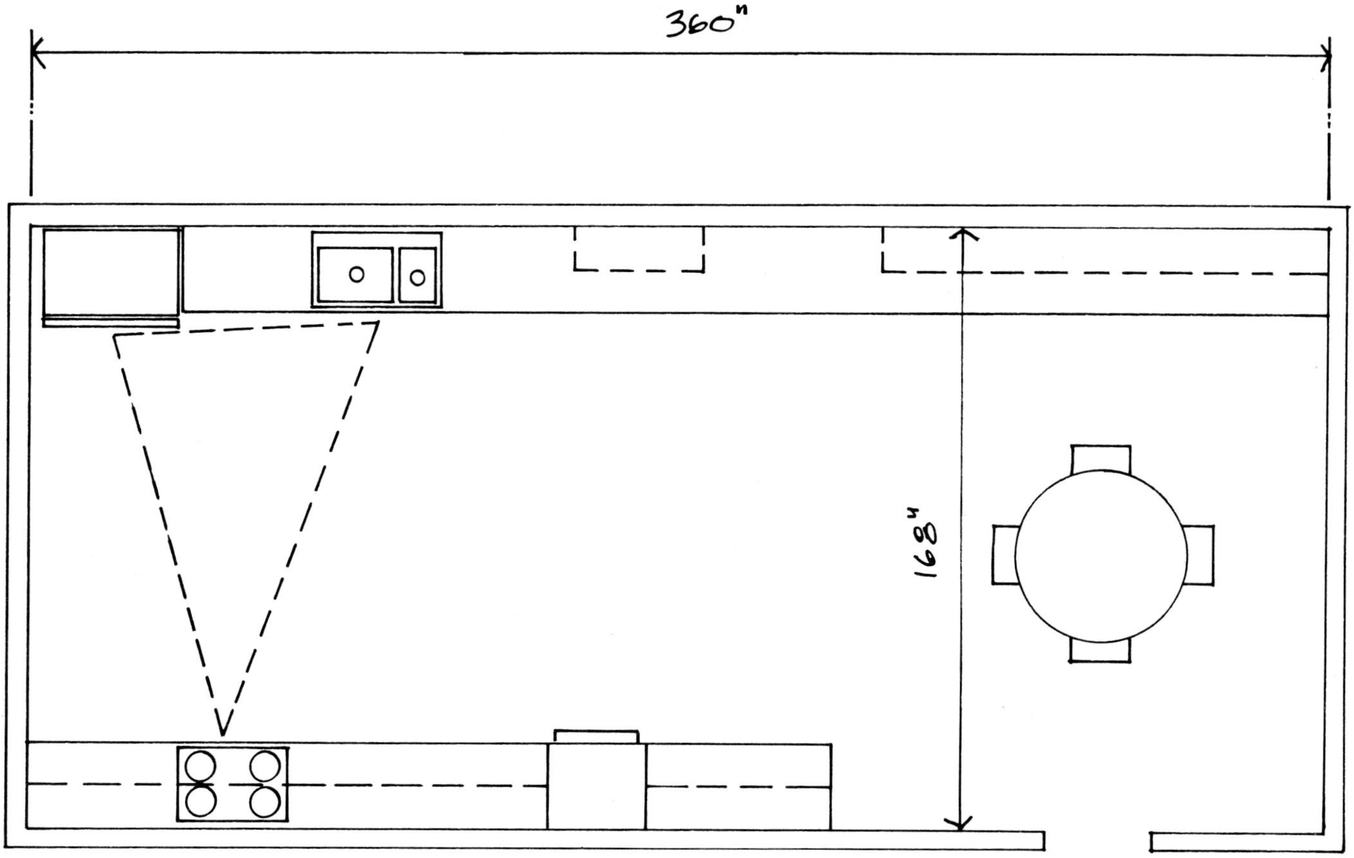

360"

168"

Figure 68. Move-up two-wall kitchen with work triangle – 25.5′, base cabinet frontage – 438″, countertop surface – 462″

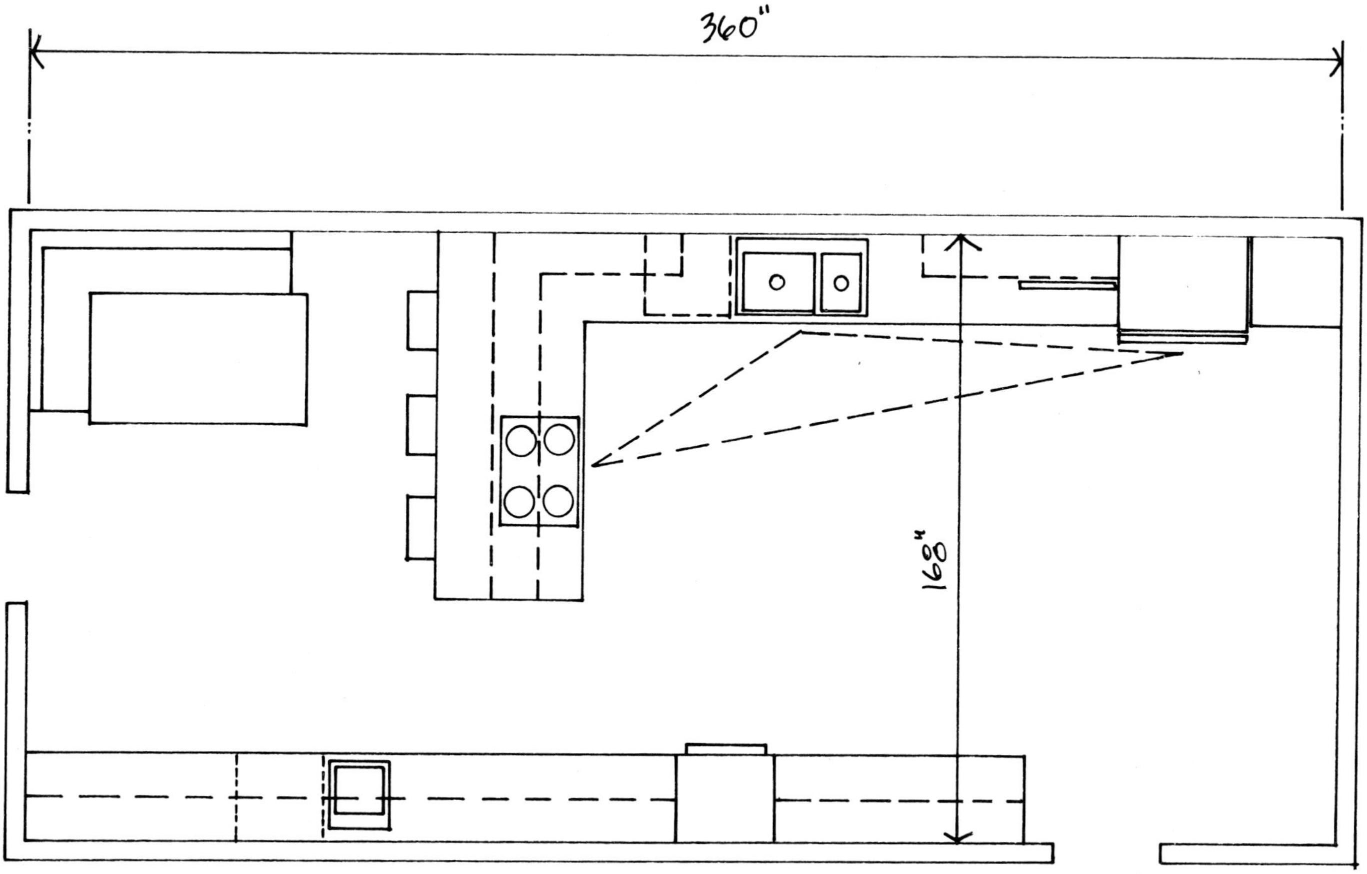

360"

168"

Figure 69. Move-up two-wall kitchen (revised) with work triangle – 28′, base cabinet frontage – 432″, countertop surface – 408″

on countertops that can be lowered to the 29- to 31-inch heights required for the handicapped. Front controls are recommended.

If a cook top is used, ovens can then be installed at a more convenient height with the most-used shelf 31 inches from the floor, lower than average, but above the height of the all-in-one range.

Self-cleaning ovens are desirable.

Hoods are important for ventilation and light. A cook top with a down-draft is preferable to a regular hood, provided sufficient light is directed to the work surface.

Install the microwave at counter height, not in the wall at eye level. Controls should be on the side, not the top. Again, electronic controls make life easier for the arthritic.

Sinks

The average sink installed on a 36-inch counter is impractical for a wheelchair occupant, who needs a shallow model at a 29- to 31-inch height. In building for the elderly, leave the sink at the standard height, but set pipes off to the rear. Lower the waste connection to less than 15 inches from the floor, so that it functions properly with a lowered sink.

To adapt the sink for a wheelchair occupant, lower it to the 29-to 31-inch height, and remove the doors under the sink so that the occupant can roll under it. When pipes are set off to the rear, this adaptation is more easily handled. Wrap pipes with insulation to prevent burns.

Spray hoses and instant hot water are welcome conveniences.

Dishwashers

Install a typical front-loading dishwasher. It should have racks that pull out independently with silverware holder and soap dispenser in the door. Install it by the sink, just as in other kitchens, with enough room to load and unload. Again, electronic controls across the front facilitate use.

Lighting and Ventilation

Effective work light is imperative for kitchens for the elderly, and the same principles used in installing any kitchen lighting apply. Position the light switches, however, 6 inches lower than usual, allowing the wheelchair occupant to see them. (Install all controls for security, radio, and intercoms 6 inches lower than normal, as well.)

Install a wall fan that a wheelchair occupant can control for ventilation, if a downdraft cook top is not used. A ceiling fan is also a good idea because it provides cooling with some ventilation and is easily operated from a wall switch.

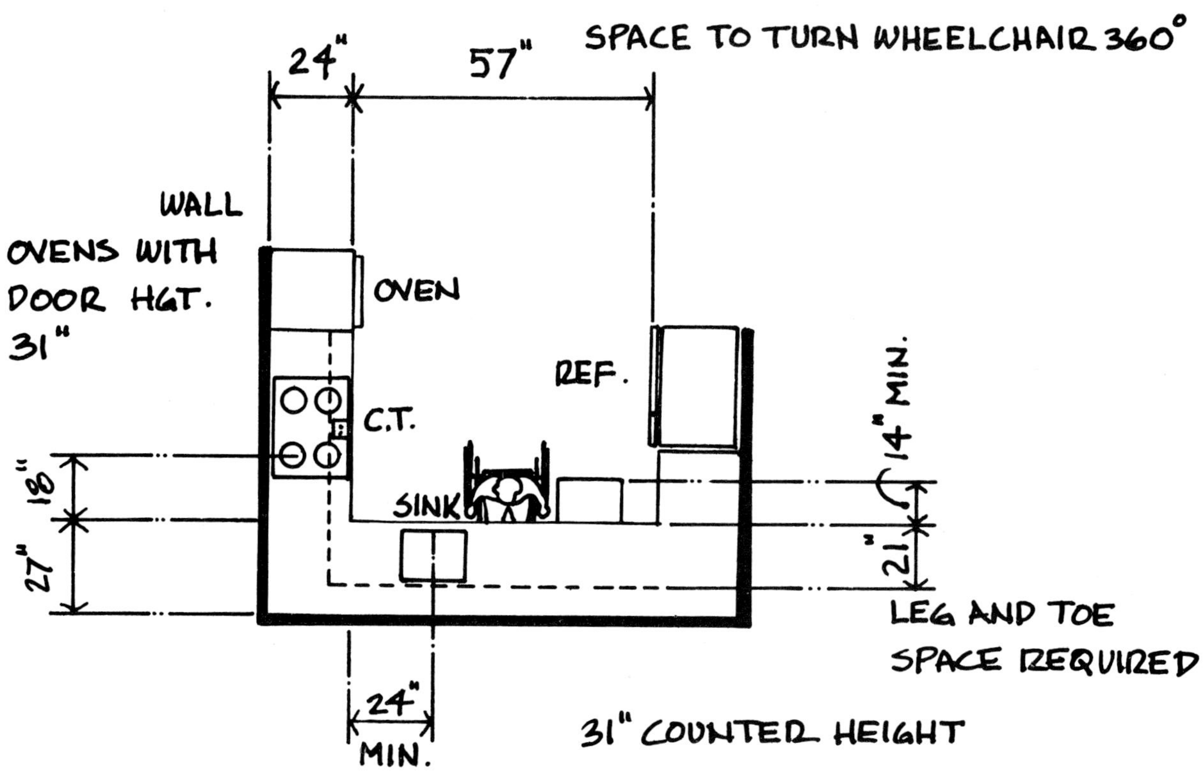

Figure 73. Specifications for kitchen dimensions that accommodate a wheelchair

Due to a production error, the following revisions to **Kitchens** have been issued:

Page 36 — The last paragraph in the first column should read:

> The maximum HVI rating for sones is 8 for a kitchen hood with up to 500-CFM capacity. Hood fans should be exhausted through a duct to the outside. Non-ducted hoods can remove odors but...

Page 43 — The caption for Figure 61 should read:

> **Figure 61. Basic one-wall kitchen (revised) with work triangle - 23′6″, base cabinet frontage - 90″, countertop surface - 186″**

Page 49 — Insert revised page.

Page 55 — Insert revised page.

Page 59 — Transpose captions for 77 and 78.

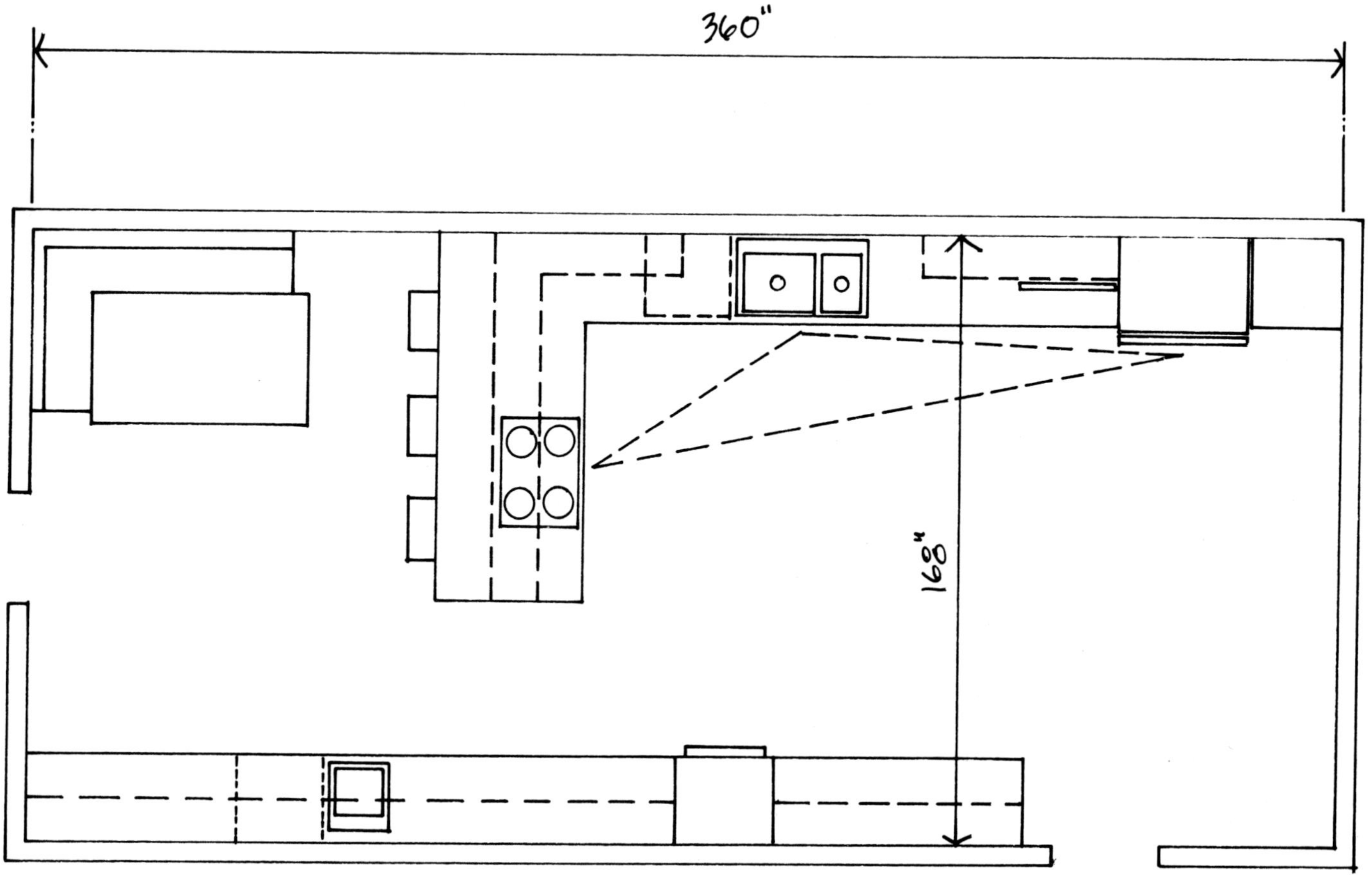

360"

168"

Figure 68. Move-up two-wall kitchen with work triangle – 25.5′, base cabinet frontage – 438″, countertop surface – 462″

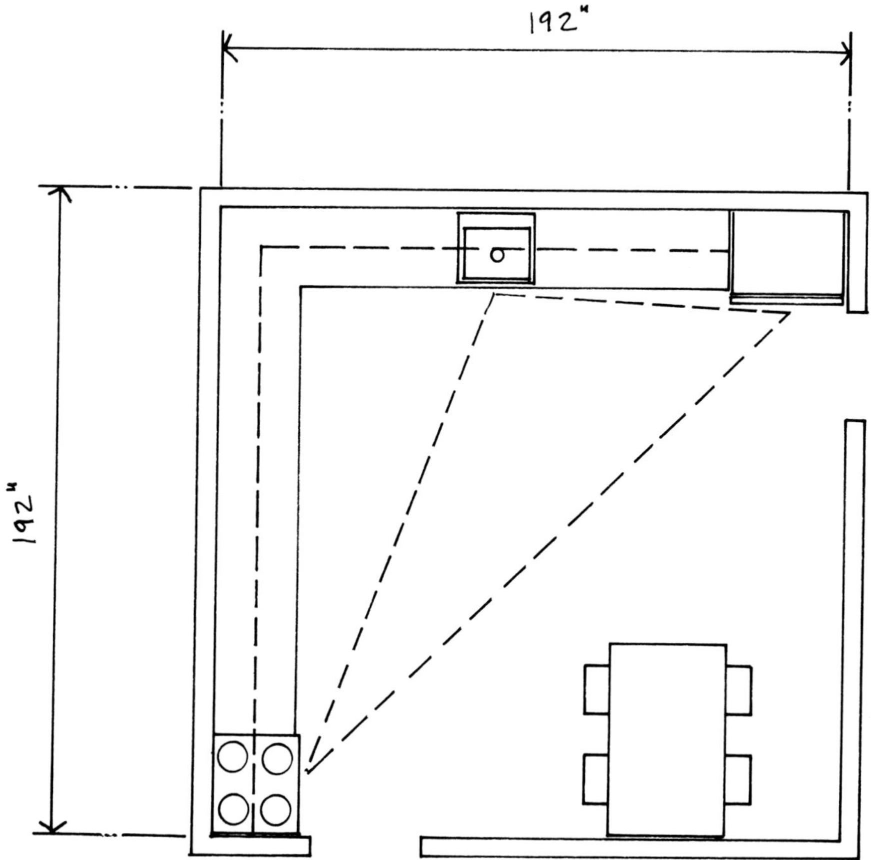

Figure 69. Move-up two-wall kitchen (revised) with work triangle – 28′, base cabinet frontage – 432″, countertop surface – 408″

the refrigerator and the sink. (See Figure 69.)

Allow 15 inches between the dishwasher and the return of the cabinet peninsula. The peninsula is large enough for eating as well as for the cook top. It is all one height, suitable for bar stools, so that two or three can use it for meals. Install a banquette and table along the end by the family room, with a chandelier over the table.

Opposite, place an entertainment area with a second, auxiliary sink, a small, under-cabinet refrigerator, bar, and cabinets for storage. Add a wine rack in this area, which is now adjacent to the family room and closer to the living room and the pool area.

Lighting a room like this takes careful thought to provide for aesthetics and practicality. Use under-cabinet lighting for the work area and the bar. Provide the overall lighting through recessed spots. Recessing the spots lights up the entire room, without interfering with the chandelier in the eating area. Since this home is a traditional one, obvious spots are out of place. (See Chapter 11.)

A downdraft cook top, easily vented to the outside with a hood over the ovens, also vented to the outside, provides ventilation.

The unusually large kitchen in this example presents one assortment of problems to resolve. A smaller corridor kitchen presents other problems.

One-Wall

An extended work triangle presents a great challenge. In the sample (Figure 70), the kitchen is 7 feet X 20 feet, 6 inches, with a work triangle of 27 feet, 6 inches—much too large.

Switching the sink and the cook top reduces the triangle to 23 feet, which saves steps. The width of the room is just enough to permit changing this arrangement to make it more convenient.

For better design, include counter space and the refrigerator in one end of the room. Install a pantry where the refrigerator was. Add the ovens next to it. On the opposite wall, add a 2-foot storage wall. Place a microwave in the mixing center. (See Figure 71.)

Alternative Designs

Most kitchens pose different design possibilities. Using the templates provided and arranging the appliances in various positions on a floor plan suggests variations. It is easy to see, for example, that an additional foot from the family room enables liberal passageway and a small counter for planning in the kitchen.

Subtracting feet is just as desirable as adding them if it reduces the work triangle to manageable size. This might, for example, enlarge the dining room enough for a table for eight, instead of one for six.

Offer as many of the new amenities as possible in the move-up kitchen. Some suggestions follow:

- Two-door refrigerator/freezer with electronic controls
- Multimode cook top
- Multimode oven
- Barbecue unit
- Built-in microwave
- Storage walls and pantry units
- Double or triple sinks
- Electronic faucets
- Instant hot-water dispensers
- Adjustable-height faucets
- Accessory sinks
- Accessory refrigerators in bar areas
- Built-in appliance cabinets
- Desk/planning centers

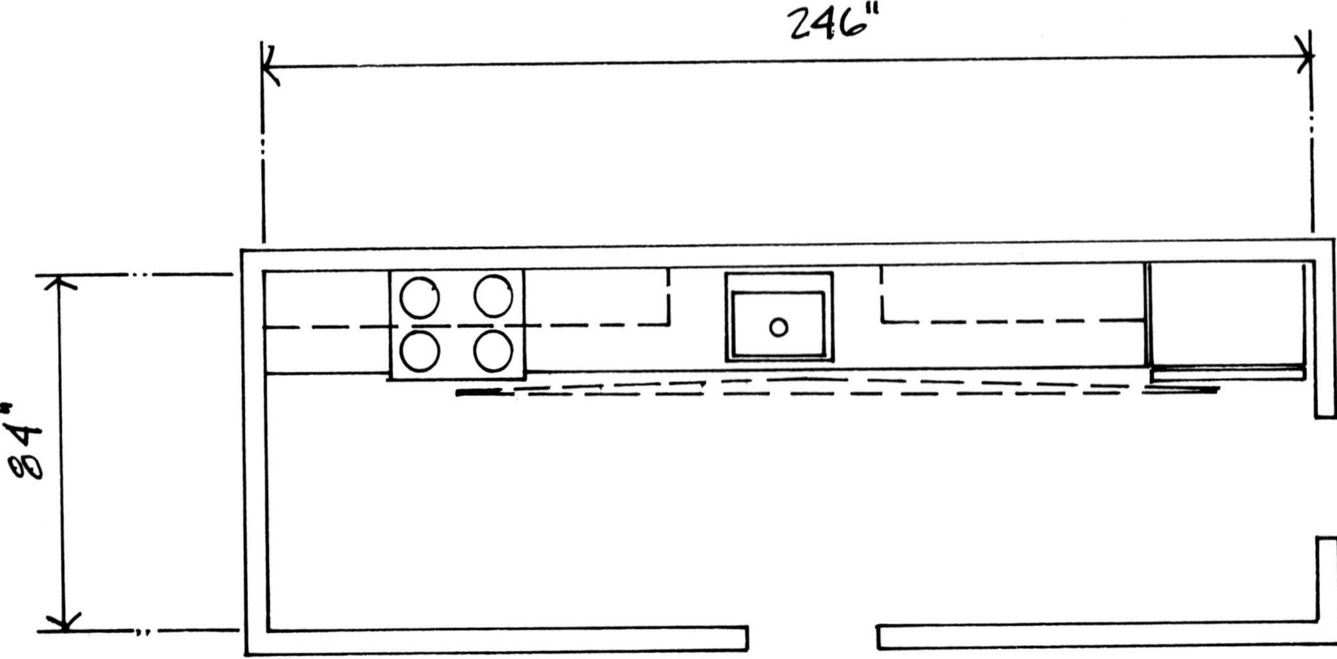

Figure 70. Move-up one-wall kitchen with work triangle – 29′, base cabinet frontage – 12′, countertop surface – 12′ 6″

Cabinets should include such features as the following:

- Cutlery drawers
- Tray cabinets
- Built-in waste containers
- Lazy susan/drum carousels
- Vacuum/broom storage cabinets

Other design ideas to add sales appeal are as follows:

- Bay windows
- Skylights
- Window walls
- Door panels on appliances
- Chandeliers
- Handsome soffit treatments
- Built-in refrigerators
- Ceramic tile
- Walk-in pantry

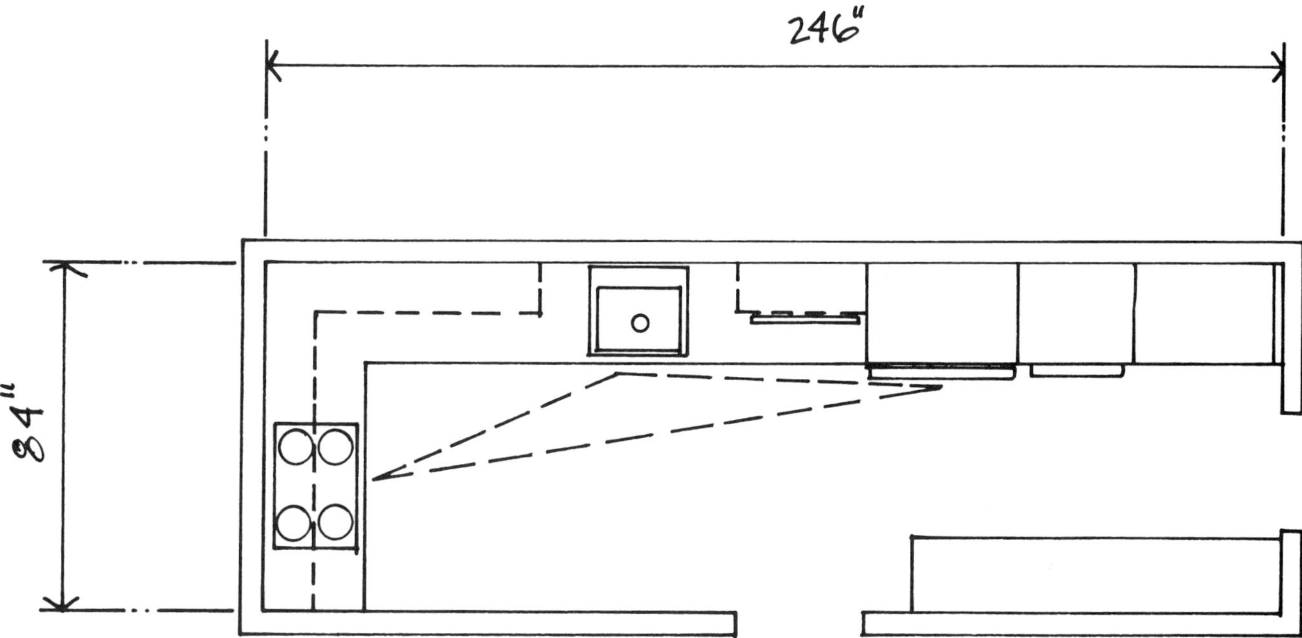

Figure 71. Move-up one-wall kitchen (revised) with work triangle – 22′, base cabinet frontage – 12′, countertop surface – 10′9″

Chapter 10

Designs for the Elderly and Handicapped

Between 20 and 40 million people in the nation are either handicapped or have some physical limitations (National Association of Home Builders 1985). With the elderly population the fastest-growing segment in the country, these numbers will increase drastically in the next decades.

Building adaptable kitchens for older people, therefore, makes sense. These kitchens are designed to enable people to better cope with their limitations.

The elderly population is not necessarily handicapped, but kitchens that are adaptable for use by those with limitations, such as arthritis or poor eyesight, are desirable. Such kitchens can then be adapted for wheelchair occupants or others with handicaps easier than can standard kitchens. (See Figure 72.)

Builders targeting the elderly market can plan adaptable kitchens with little initial trouble, but redesigning kitchens to accommodate a wheelchair occupant, for example, is expensive.

The Basic Kitchen Plan

The basic rules of good kitchen planning apply to kitchens for the elderly and handicapped just as much as they do for other segments of the market. The work centers must form a triangle, and the most efficient kitchens are the U-shaped and the L-shaped ones. Corridor kitchens and one-wall kitchens can be used, but present greater problems, especially for those in wheelchairs.

Each work center has a recommended minimum amount of counter space. The absolute minimum of counter space required is 72 inches (National Kitchen and Bath Association 1984).

Certain space adjustments should be made initially, so that the kitchen can be made readily accessible to someone in a wheelchair at a later date (Figure 73).

Doorways must have clearances of 32 inches or more. This includes the 2 inches needed for an opened door. (See Figure 74.)

A wheelchair requires a center turning space of 4-1/2 to 5-1/2 feet. This amount of space must be available in the center of the kitchen to permit the occupant to turn to reach all appliances.

Standard 36-inch counters are too high for most people to reach from a wheelchair. The most practical height is 31 inches (29-1/2 inches from the floor), which provides a work height that is easily manageable for most tasks. Someone in a wheelchair, however, cannot chop or beat at that height and needs a 27-inch height surface for this type of work. A pull-out table or board lowered to this height or one that can be adjusted later is a good solution.

Countertop design offers many options for adaptability. For example, a length of counter at a seating height of 31 inches provides a convenience not only for the handicapped but for everyone because many people like to sit while they work. Include an overhang of at least 12 inches for knee room. Place this counter in the mixing center, adjacent to the refrigerator and sink, to eliminate steps.

Install a pull-out breadboard at the 31-inch height by the range/cook top.

If space and kitchen configuration allow, install a folding table at the 31-inch height.

Cabinets

Although a woman of average height can reach up to 72 inches, the elderly are not as flexible.

To accommodate the elderly, add cabinets and closets with pull-out drawers and shelves in the base cabinets in addition to overhead storage. Lazy susan installations and narrow pantry walls are practical. Pull-out bins for pots, pans, food storage, waste baskets, and cleaning supplies make using the kitchen easier. Install cutlery and pull-out drawers for linens, tableware, and other storage, as well as lazy susan/

drum carousels for corners and other cabinets.

Appliances

Unless appliances are specially designed for the handicapped, those that are most suitable for the elderly serve the handicapped as well.

When adapting homes or units for the blind, provide Braille panels for some appliances. These are overlays for the control panel with microcomputer touch controls that can also be read by the sighted.

Refrigerators

Install refrigerators with side-by-side doors; automatic ice and water dispensers are most convenient. The third door, a shallow, refrigerated storage compartment, is also handy. The refrigerator should be frost-free; revolving or slide-out shelves are desirable.

Cook Tops, Ranges, and Ovens

The cooking center should have front controls, so they can be easily reached. Electronic controls are simpler for the arthritic to use, but make sure these are readable by those with poor eyesight.

Include enough room beside the oven door for a wheelchair occupant—a minimum of 32 inches. A pull-out breadboard at a 31-inch height beside the oven is helpful.

The set-in range is preferable to a standard slide-in one, because the standard 36-inch height is adjustable by lowering the base height for a wheelchair occupant. Controls should be in front where they can be easily read. Burners should be staggered, if possible, so that the user does not have to reach across the front burners to get to the back ones.

Cook tops offer great versatility. They can be placed

Courtesy Whirlpool

Figure 72. This adaptable kitchen features a cook top that accommodates a wheelchair, a mirror above the cook top so that anyone seated can see into the pots, convenient open storage, accessible vent control, and an oven at a height suitable for those seated or standing.

on countertops that can be lowered to the 29- to 31-inch heights required for the handicapped. Front controls are recommended.

If a cook top is used, ovens can then be installed at a more convenient height with the most-used shelf 31 inches from the floor, lower than average, but above the height of the all-in-one range.

Self-cleaning ovens are desirable.

Hoods are important for ventilation and light. A cook top with a down-draft is preferable to a regular hood, provided sufficient light is directed to the work surface.

Install the microwave at counter height, not in the wall at eye level. Controls should be on the side, not the top. Again, electronic controls make life easier for the arthritic.

Sinks

The average sink installed on a 36-inch counter is impractical for a wheelchair occupant, who needs a shallow model at a 29- to 31-inch height. In building for the elderly, leave the sink at the standard height, but set pipes off to the rear. Lower the waste connection to less than 15 inches from the floor, so that it functions properly with a lowered sink.

To adapt the sink for a wheelchair occupant, lower it to the 29-to 31-inch height, and remove the doors under the sink so that the occupant can roll under it. When pipes are set off to the rear, this adaptation is more easily handled. Wrap pipes with insulation to prevent burns.

Spray hoses and instant hot water are welcome conveniences.

Dishwashers

Install a typical front-loading dishwasher. It should have racks that pull out independently with silverware holder and soap dispenser in the door. Install it by the sink, just as in other kitchens, with enough room to load and unload. Again, electronic controls across the front facilitate use.

Lighting and Ventilation

Effective work light is imperative for kitchens for the elderly, and the same principles used in installing any kitchen lighting apply. Position the light switches, however, 6 inches lower than usual, allowing the wheelchair occupant to see them. (Install all controls for security, radio, and intercoms 6 inches lower than normal, as well.)

Install a wall fan that a wheelchair occupant can control for ventilation, if a downdraft cook top is not used. A ceiling fan is also a good idea because it provides cooling with some ventilation and is easily operated from a wall switch.

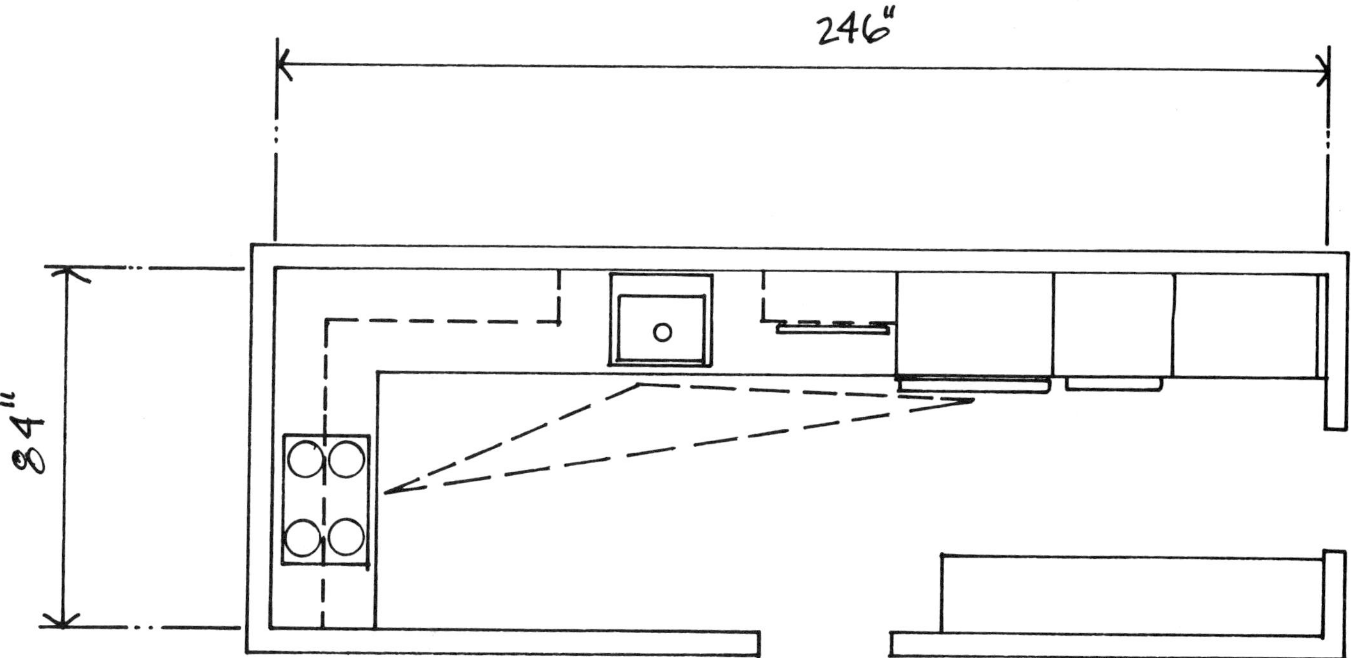

Figure 73. Specifications for kitchen dimensions that accommodate a wheelchair

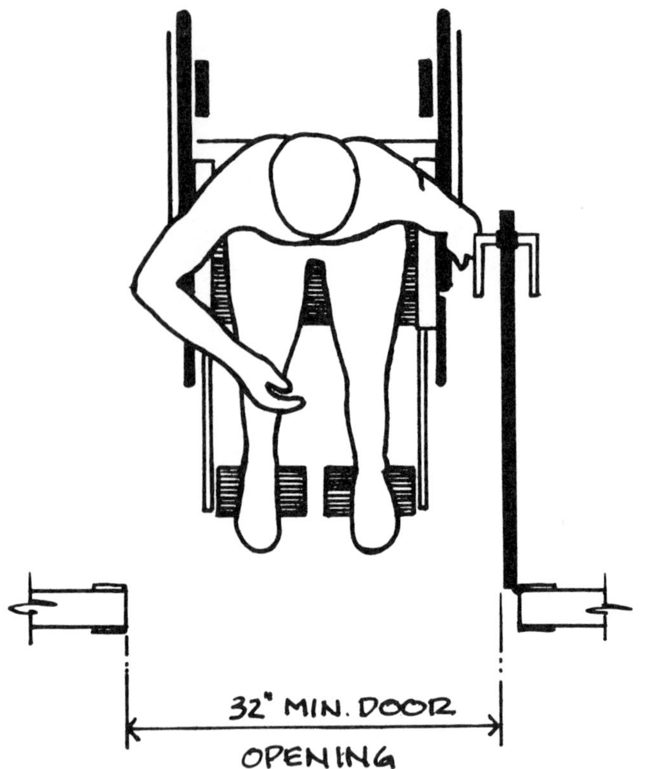

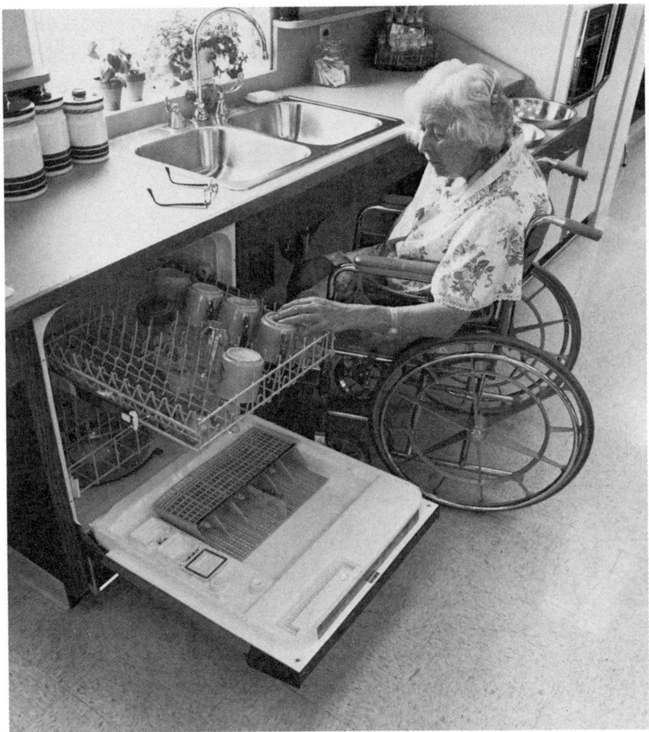

Courtesy Whirlpool

Figure 75. This sink is accessible to the wheelchair-bound.

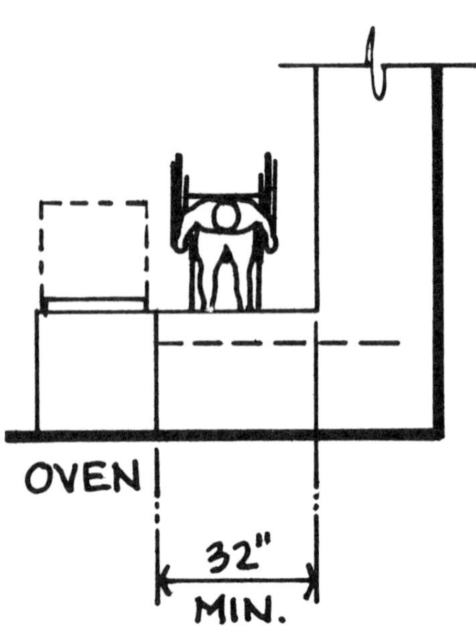

Figure 74. Allow 32 inches of space beside the oven for a wheelchair. A doorway must be 32 inches wide to accommodate a wheelchair.

Chapter 11

Design Themes, Color, and Texture

Once an efficient work triangle is established and appliances are chosen, an appropriate design theme completes the kitchen.

A knowledge of the standard types of decor and their distinguishing characteristics enhances your ability to create marketable kitchens or provide guidance to a kitchen designer. This chapter illustrates different design themes used in one sample kitchen and discusses color and texture to familiarize you with these elements.

Variations and adaptations abound in the design world. No kitchen is pure stylistically. Good design effectively combines various elements to create the desired feeling without sacrificing efficiency. Avoid fads; good design is fairly timeless and does not become dated.

First you must decide the type of mood or look that is desired. Is it to be a colonial or European-style kitchen? Is the Mission look popular in the area? Consider that a traditional colonial home adapts well to traditional kitchens or European ones, but southwestern, Spanish-influenced architecture works better with a Mission-inspired treatment or a contemporary design.

In addition, color and texture provide interest and create a mood. Exciting uses of each beautify your designs.

When the type of decor has been selected, then all of the decorative elements should be determined to expedite installation. Special finishes, custom cabinets, and out-of-the-ordinary materials for floorings require extra time to procure. Give the designer plenty of time to ensure a timely, well-coordinated job. As any builder who has suffered through the delivery of the wrong sized windows or a short shipment of brick can understand, something always can and will go wrong. Planning and ordering ahead are the only prevention for delays and problems.

Traditional

Traditional kitchens often reflect standard Williamsburg style, although colonial influences are many and varied. This style has the formal balance that distinguishes a traditional room and can be dressed up or down.

Many styles of kitchen cabinets coordinate with this theme. Cabinetry may have raised panels, recessed panels, cathedral arches, or simply have a tongue-and-groove construction.

Typical woods are oak, cherry, and maple. The tones of the wood are medium to medium dark, with a soft patina for a rich and warm effect. The black glass fronts of ovens blend well with these woods.

Countertops can be laminated, Corian, butcher block, or tile. Wood trim on the tile adds to the effect. Colors should blend well with the wood tones and are often the typical Williamsburg colors of cranberry, greyed blues and greens, and definite golds. Rust tones also work well.

Soffits can be boxed in or open with gallery rails on the cabinets. Woodwork can be stained to match the cabinets or painted in a darker tone of the wall color. Beams are often used to add ceiling interest and can provide useful hanging space for pots or baskets. Wood trim helps carry out the traditional theme.

Floors in the traditional kitchen are vinyl in wood, brick, or stone patterns, polished wood, antique brick, or stone. The floor tone should be a medium color.

Walls are painted or papered in a traditionally patterned paper. Painting most walls, then papering the area between the cabinets and above the open soffit provides additional interest.

Country

One of the warmest, coziest looks, the country kitchen, evokes images of hanging baskets, bread baking in the oven, and pets sleeping on rag rugs. Actu-

Mission kitchen

Country kitchen

Traditional kitchen

French provincial kitchen

Contemporary kitchen

Courtesy Don O'Connor

Figures 76. One kitchen in five different styles

ally, country influences stem from many countries, such as Spain, Mexico, and France. But most consumers think of country style as early American, rustic, and informal.

This style emphasizes natural materials, and it is not formally balanced like the traditional kitchen. Cabinets need not be symmetrical, and off-balanced groupings are used.

Cabinetry for the country kitchen is usually pine, cherry, or maple, finished in lighter tones or even left unfinished. Tan or grey tones work well, and painted cabinets in fairly strong colors are typical of the style. Painted cabinets, however, should probably be reserved for custom work. Cabinets are tongue and groove or flat surfaced. Panels are also used. Use wrought iron, hammered metal, or white ceramic for hardware.

Ceilings with heavy, rough beams belong in the country kitchen, as do wrought iron hanging racks for pots and pans.

Countertops blend well in laminates with wood finishes or in colors that coordinate with the cabinets. Natural woods are ideal; tile and stone go with the rustic look.

Walls may be paneled with flat paneling to match the cabinets or painted. Stenciling on walls is also typical of the theme but is an expensive custom touch. Stenciled borders in wallpapers are available, however, as are country motif papers.

Use these in small doses, such as on one wall or between cabinets. A natural brick wall adds an informal note and sets the mood of the room.

Early American floors were wood, of course, and sometimes were painted. A wood- or brick-design vinyl or wide-board wooden floor works well in the country kitchen. Brick, stone, and tile are also appropriate.

Do not combine too many different materials, particularly in a small room. The effect could be confusing.

Colors are warm, and the warm tones of the natural materials blend well with honey colors. The clean look of blue and white is also highly effective in a rustic kitchen, as are many of the traditional tile colors.

Mission

Born of the Spanish and Indian cultures of the West, Mission style is all too often thought of as heavy, dark, and ponderous. In good interpretations today, however, this style has a warmth and friendliness that is highly appealing.

This is another country style and is generally popular in the West and Southwest. It works well in a ranch house or a home with a sense of nearness to the earth. Custom-designed kitchens of this type might have stuccoed walls with wooden beams and trim. Traditionally, such kitchens were whitewashed and the beams darkened from smoke.

Today's versions use Spanish, Mexican, Indian, and

Courtesy St. Charles

Figure 77. Traditional kitchen

Courtesy Sub-Zero Freezer Company

Figure 78. Country kitchen

Courtesy Armstrong World Industries, Inc.

Figure 79. Mission kitchen

Courtesy Wood-Mode Cabinetry

Figure 80. French provincial kitchen

South American motifs. Cabinetry is in medium dark, mellow tones in walnut, oak, or pine. Glass doors with lattice work coordinate well. Open shelves with gallery rails and spindles used as trim and room dividers carry out the theme.

Cut-out effects on aprons, exposed beams, and stone walls all work well.

The ideal kitchen in this style has a fireplace, but you can create this effect with an arched niche for a cook top, the arch concealing the venting.

Brick floors, tile countertops, inserts of butcher block for chopping, and copper for accessory sinks are all complementary to this style.

White walls, sand- or stucco-finished, or white-washed stone coordinate well. Tiles on sections of the walls match the countertops or repeat a design theme; wooden edging on the tile counters, wrought iron, and wooden or Mexican tin fixtures all contribute to the look.

Colors for this style are the sand tones of the desert, Indian reds, and black and white with red. Or try a terra-cotta floor and terra-cotta tile counter with tans and browns.

French Provincial

At one time, French provincial or an adaptation of it was the popular leader in kitchen design, as well as in furniture choice. It is still a handsome style that can be used to great advantage.

French Provincial is essentially a country look, a warm, informal treatment. Not as rough hewn in feeling as the country kitchen, it uses cabinetry with a more finished appearance, usually characterized by a molding in the same color as the rest of the cabinet or a contrasting color. French provincial lends itself to painted finishes, in such colors as white with blue-grey trim. In wood finishes, the tones are warm, and the woods are usually cherry, maple, or birch.

Tile is the ideal countertop for French provincial, either on all counters or on an island or a peninsula. Tiled backsplashes and tiled walls above the counters work well in this room. Tiles can be plain or with charming botanical designs. Plain tiles combined with randomly decorated ones or with geometric borders are effective.

Laminates work well also. Countertops that are white or with edgings that match cabinet trim coordinate well with two-toned cabinets, like those that are white with blue trim.

Wallpaper with tile-like patterns is effective when ceramic tile is not called for. Or consider painting the walls and adding a wallpaper border.

Floors for this kitchen are tile, brick, slate, or vinyl (that looks like a natural material). Wood is also a good choice. French provincial has a casual look—but not rustic. It can also be quite elegant. When building in hot climates, French provincial style with its light, painted effect creates a cool feeling that is highly attractive.

Consider built-in wine racks, the addition of lozenge glass doors on some of the cabinets, and a copper hood to carry out the theme.

Pastels, such as pale, grey blues, soft yellows, greens, greys, and the blonde tones work well in these kitchens. Hardware can be iron, pewter, or hammered metals. If tiles are used, ceramic hardware that matches is a possibility.

European-Style

The clean, slick European-styled cabinetry is capturing more of the market today. It is particularly popular in the East and in urban areas, although it is used all over the country. Generally, it is considered upscale, although most manufacturers now include some version in their lines.

Cabinets are flat laminates with bands of color running horizontally. These may be wood, although metal trims are used.

The European concept in construction makes this look possible. Without the frame that is used in other types of cabinets, these have a flat, smoothly flowing effect. This also gives greater storage space on the interior, as well as more ease in using the cabinets.

Generally, colors are white, soft grey, beige, and blued white. Color accents may be hot, such as red, or soft pastels and natural tones. Edgings and trims add color touches. Color impact depends on minimalism: grey and white, beige and white, white with red flashes, white with wood trim and wood tones in the floor, or all white or grey.

Exciting textures, such as leather looks, and mosaics may be used for cabinet fronts, as well as countertops. The shine of real marble or marble laminates combines beautifully for countertops, as do tiles, slate, and granite. Laminates in the various patterns, such as millstone, marbles, granites, are exceptionally handsome.

Soffits may be open or boxed for a continuous line. A glass front cabinet adds interest.

Floors should be vinyl, tile, or slate. Wooden floors to match the wooden trim warm up the European kitchen and add a distinctive note. Tile works well with this look.

A restrained hand is the key to the successful use of this design motif. In a small area, it creates the illusion of space and size. It also seems cooler in a hot climate.

Courtesy Siematic

Figure 81. European-style kitchen

Contemporary

What is contemporary? Is it Art Deco, high-tech, or a combination of both? A bit of Oriental? The European look? It is any of these. Primarily, it is a clean, uncluttered look.

Colors should be contrasting darks and lights. Woods and laminates can be used together. Marble countertops work well, as do Corian or color-cored laminates. Edges should be rounded. Boxy shapes work well. Cabinets feature integral pulls, rather than hardware, to avoid any disruption of the solid mass.

Courtesy Wilsonart

Figure 82. Contemporary kitchen

Other Design Styles

There are many design variations to use. The ranch style, for instance, is a rough-hewn approach to a country kitchen. Or a Victorian kitchen uses traditional cabinetry in darker tones, colored glass fronts, and heavy moldings. Most of these are custom-built kitchens and require design refinements that are the specialty of the interior designer or kitchen specialist.

Color

Color evokes emotions and ideas. Colors make us happy; they excite us, calm us; they create a homey feeling; they project cleanliness; they exercise a profound influence over our lives, yet generally we are unconscious of their effect on our psyches.

The study of color is part of the interior designer's art, and their proper use is a measure of the skill of the designer. Generally, the builder is wise to rely on a professional for the decorative part of the kitchen, as well as for its proper layout. Ultimately, however, it is the builder who must agree to the designer's ideas and accept responsibility for the success of the decor.

Since model homes must appeal to the widest number of buyers, the kitchen has to have broad acceptance. A model is no place for wild experimentation but is the place for using color to enhance your design. Cool colors, blues and greens, add a sense of serenity and enlarge a space or make a ceiling seem higher. Cool colors work well with white, such as in a cool blue and white or green and white room.

Use the cool colors to create both traditional and contemporary kitchens. For instance, you can create a country kitchen with medium-toned cabinets, accents of blue and white tile, with butcher block countertops and a copper hood. Blue or green make handsome accents in a stark white kitchen using laminated cabinets.

The warm colors are based on reds and yellows. These give a cozier, livelier atmosphere. Used on walls, they make the space seem smaller. The darker the tone, the more it contracts the space.

In the average kitchen, warm colors overall may make the room seem confined. Warm colors are better used as accents in cool-colored rooms. Reds and oranges enliven the dramatic look of European and Art Deco designs.

The neutral tones of nature, wood tones, and the soft shades of sand and brick lend themselves to a variety of decors and combine well with cool or warm tones. In general, neutrals form the base for the kitchen and are used for the floor, cabinets, and walls.

Floors are traditionally the darkest element in a room; the walls are medium and the ceiling, light. Since wooden cabinets are generally darker and also give a feeling of weight, the floor in the kitchen is usually a medium tone, the walls behind the cabinets are also medium, and the ceiling is light. Ceiling and walls can be the same color, which has the effect of raising the ceiling height, just as a lighter ceiling does.

Dark color absorbs light, while light color reflects it. Since good lighting is essential in the kitchen, try to reflect light in your design. Dark floors and dark cabinets tend to reduce reflected light, unless additional light sources are provided.

Although a pure white kitchen is extremely good looking, the use of a combination of colors is more appealing to the general public. For instance, a kitchen with white laminated cabinets, walls, and countertops might have a warm, pink-beige tone for its base cabinets and a deeper shade of the same beige for the floor tile. The use of color, in this case, reduces the "institutional" look.

A country kitchen with warm-colored wooden cabinets, on the other hand, benefits from the use of white countertops and a blue- and white-patterned wallpaper with a wooden or vinyl brick floor. A white ceiling and lighting fixtures in brass and milk glass add to the appeal. The blue and white cool the room down, giving it a restful feeling.

Texture

Texture is just as important as color in the design of the kitchen. It creates interest and prevents monotony. Textures can be gentle, as in wood and laminate, or they can be strong, as in brick and tile. Balancing a dominant texture against a recessive one is pleasing to the eye.

Oven fronts are of sleek materials, often black glass today. Sinks are shiny stainless steel or ceramic. Countertops are of generally smooth materials, either laminates, tile, marble, or wood. Yet all of these materials have different textures.

Texture, like color, must be used carefully. As in most things, more is not necessarily better. Imagine the confusion created by combining a textured floor, such as a colonial slate vinyl, with wooden-paneled cabinets, a floral wallpaper, and tile-trimmed countertops.

In a small kitchen, you must coordinate textures to avoid busyness. For instance, the smooth look of laminated cabinets, laminated countertops and appliances with matching panel doors seems to enlarge a room. The eye is uninterrupted by changes in color and texture, giving a feeling of space—the same type of illusion created when the eye travels down an uninterrupted road into the horizon.

The European-style laminated cabinets with strips of horizontal inlay give the same effect and are warmer and more interesting because of the change in texture and color. The inlay does not disturb or interrupt the eye's horizontal path. Judicious use of a ceramic tile floor in such a room adds another texture, and used on a large expanse, it enhances the feeling of space.

Appendix 1 - Templates and Graph Paper

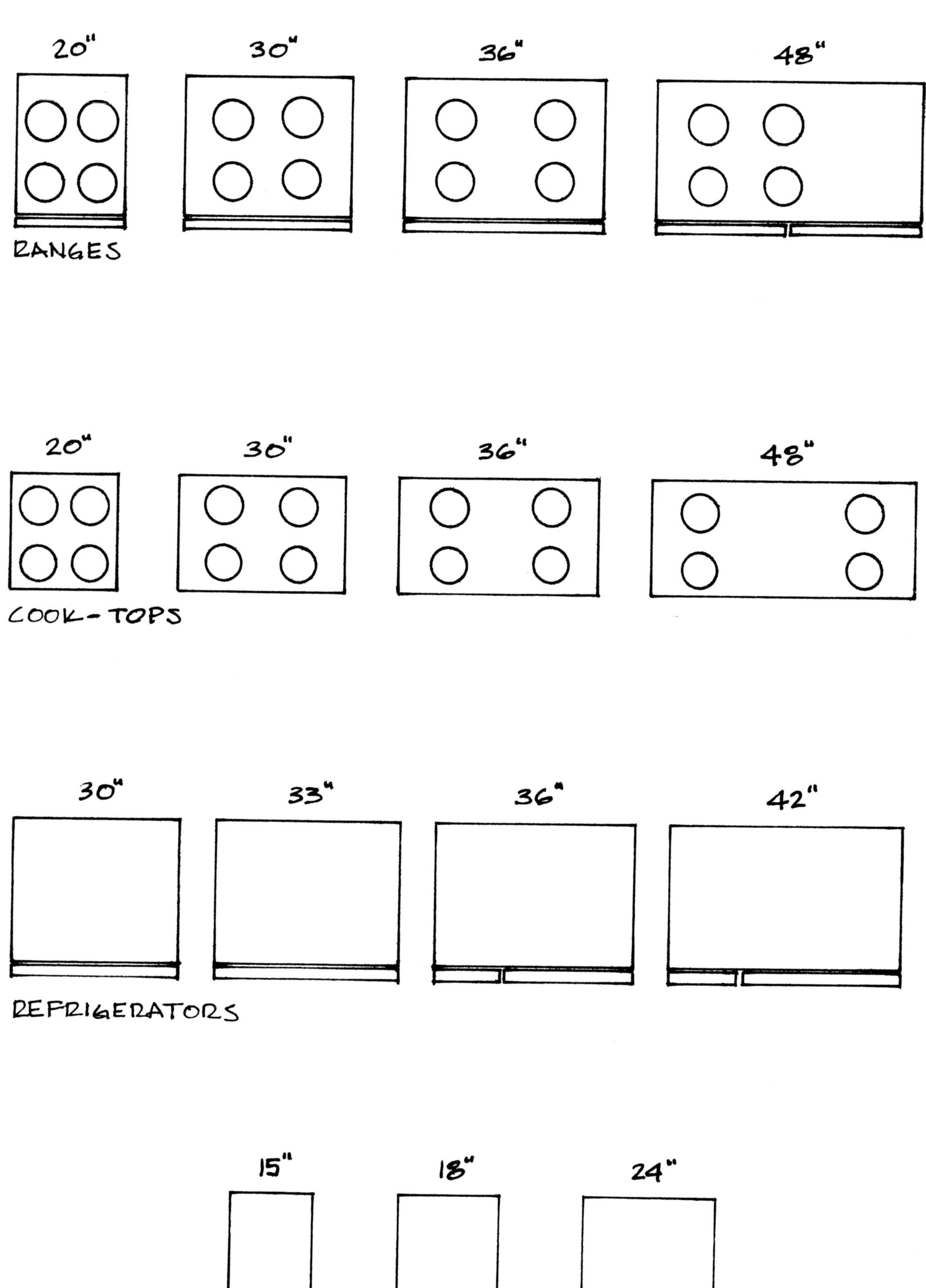
20"
30"
36"
48"
RANGES
20"
30"
36"
48"
COOK-TOPS
30"
33"
36"
42"
REFRIGERATORS
15"
18"
24"
COMPACTORS
DISHWASHER

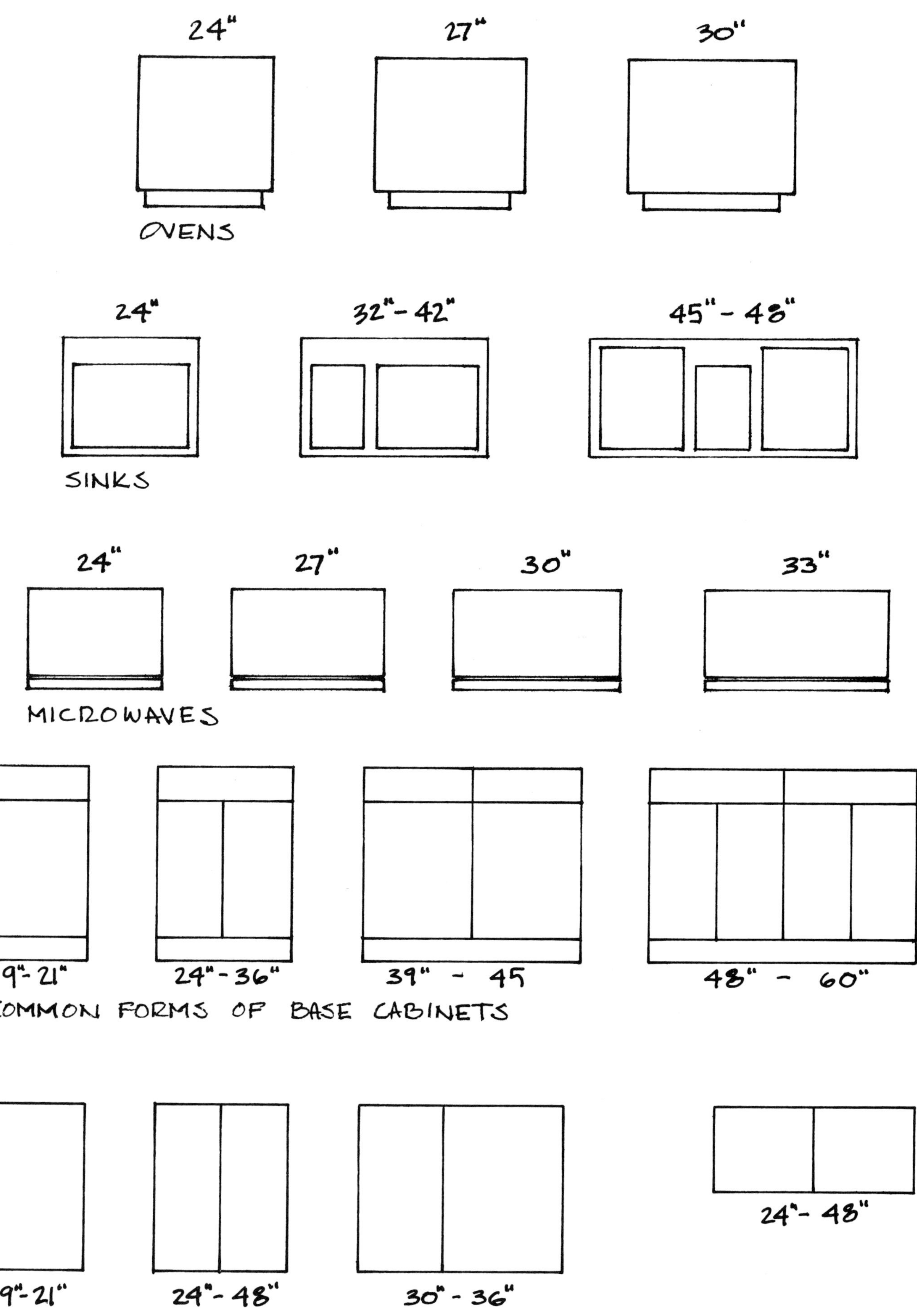
24"
27"
30"
OVENS
24"
32"-42"
45"-48"
SINKS
24"
27"
30"
33"
MICROWAVES
9"-21"
24"-36"
39" - 45
48" - 60"
COMMON FORMS OF BASE CABINETS
24"-48"
9"-21"
24"-48"
30"-36"
COMMON FORMS OF WALL CABINETS

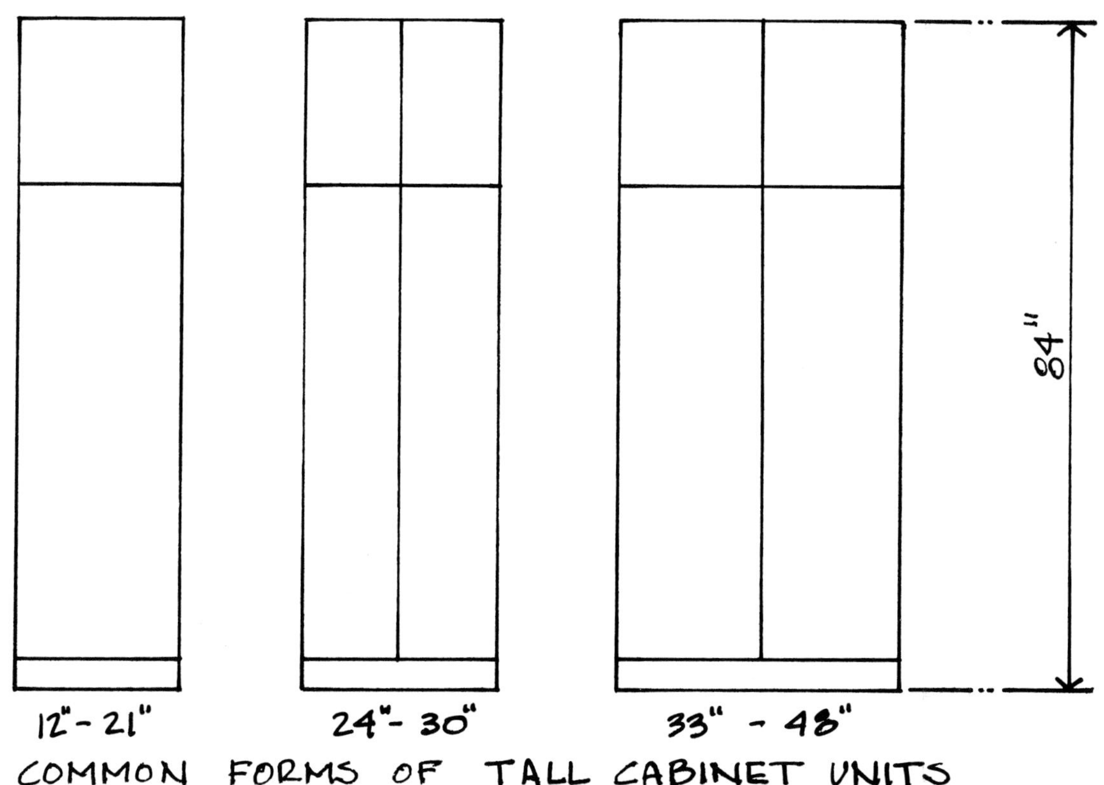

COMMON FORMS OF TALL CABINET UNITS

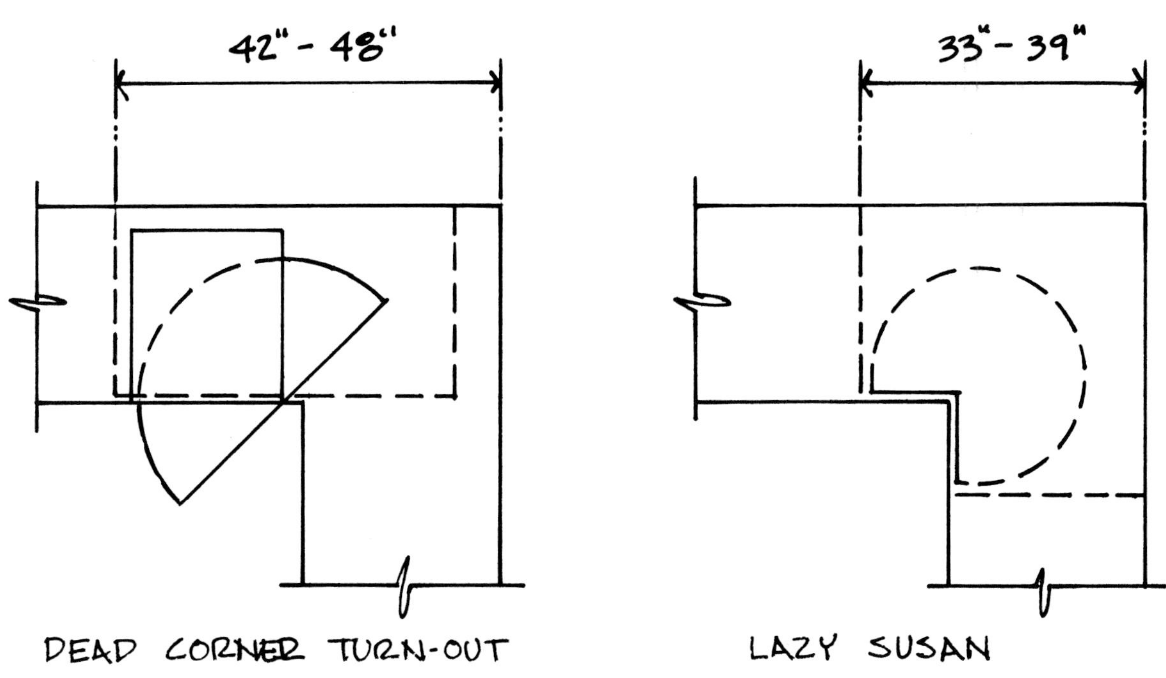

DEAD CORNER TURN-OUT

LAZY SUSAN

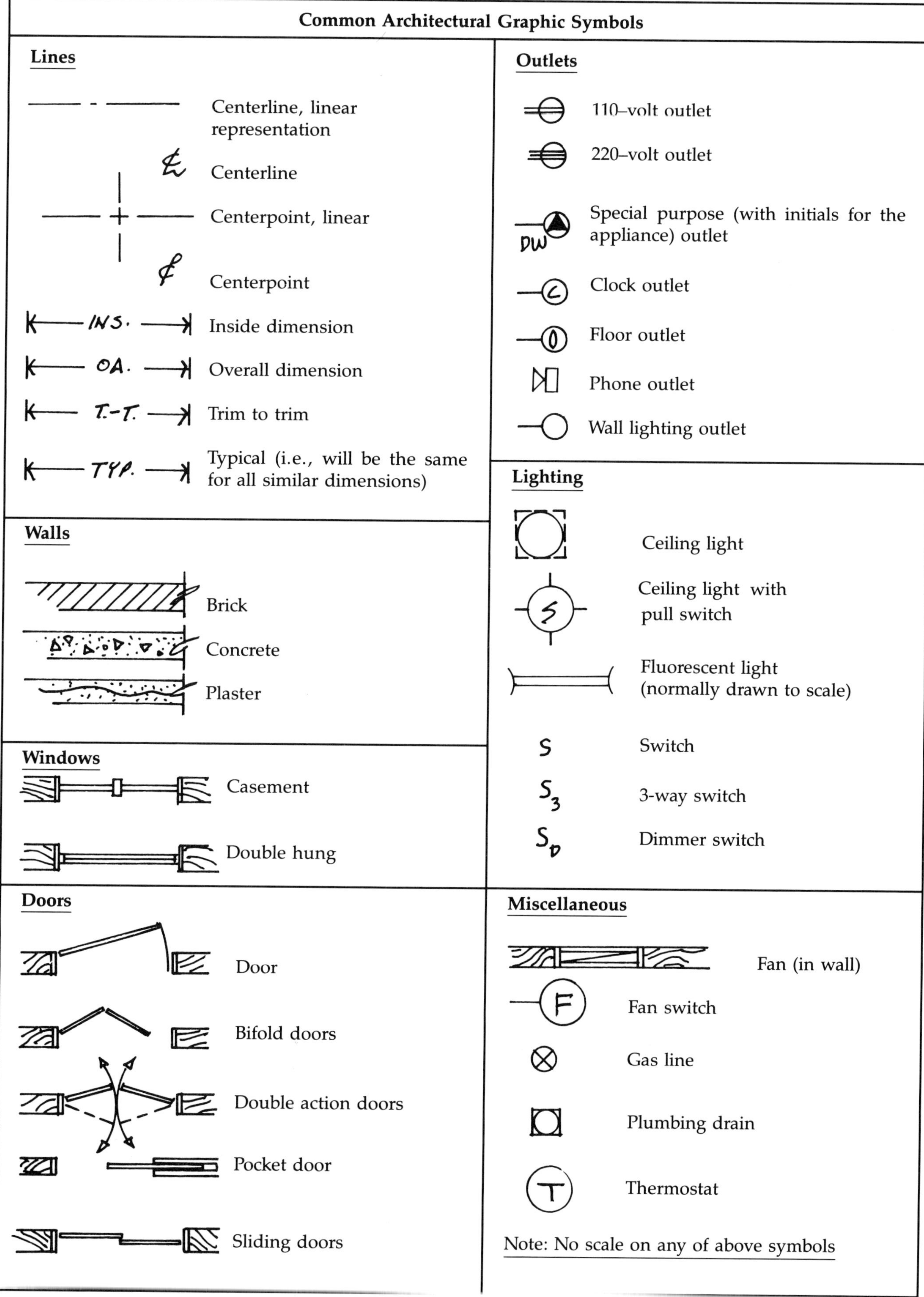
Common Architectural Graphic Symbols
Lines
Centerline, linear representation
Centerline
Centerpoint, linear
Centerpoint
INS.
Inside dimension
OA.
Overall dimension
T.-T.
Trim to trim
TYP.
Typical (i.e., will be the same for all similar dimensions)
Walls
Brick
Concrete
Plaster
Windows
Casement
Double hung
Doors
Door
Bifold doors
Double action doors
Pocket door
Sliding doors
Outlets
110–volt outlet
220–volt outlet
DW
Special purpose (with initials for the appliance) outlet
Clock outlet
Floor outlet
Phone outlet
Wall lighting outlet
Lighting
Ceiling light
Ceiling light with pull switch
Fluorescent light (normally drawn to scale)
S
Switch
S3
3-way switch
SD
Dimmer switch
Miscellaneous
Fan (in wall)
F
Fan switch
Gas line
Plumbing drain
T
Thermostat
Note: No scale on any of above symbols

References

"Consumer Kitchen Remodeling Report," *Kitchen and Bath Business* 30 (September 1984): 67-120.

National Association of Home Builders. *Decisions for the '90's.* Washington, DC: NAHB, 1985.

National Kitchen and Bath Association. *Kitchen Industry Technical Manual.* Hackettstown, NJ: NKBA, 1984.

"The Growing Importance of the Kitchen and Bath; Nationwide Builders Survey," *Kitchen and Bath News* 4 (March 1986): 51-53.

"What 1986 Buyers Want in Housing," *Professional Builder* 50 (December 1985): 66-85.

NAHB Bookstore